CANADA-U.S. RELATIONS

CANADA-U.S. RELATIONS

CARL EK

Novinka Books
New York

Senior Editors: Susan Boriotti and Donna Dennis
Coordinating Editor: Tatiana Shohov
Office Manager: Annette Hellinger
Graphics: Wanda Serrano
Editorial Production: Vladimir Klestov, Matthew Kozlowski, Tom Moceri,
　　　　　　　　　　　　Anthony T. Sovak, Alexandra Columbus and Maya Columbus
Circulation: Ave Maria Gonzalez, Vera Popovic, Luis Aviles, Raymond Davis,
　　　　　　　　Melissa Diaz and Jeannie Pappas
Marketing: Cathy DeGregory

Library of Congress Cataloging-in-Publication Data
Available Upon Request

ISBN: 1-59033-605-4.

Copyright © 2003 by Novinka Books, An Imprint of
　　　　　　　　　Nova Science Publishers, Inc.
　　　　　　　　　400 Oser Ave, Suite 1600
　　　　　　　　　Hauppauge, New York 11788-3619
　　　　　　　　　Tele. 631-231-7269　　　　　　Fax 631-231-8175
　　　　　　　　　e-mail: Novascience@earthlink.net
　　　　　　　　　Web Site: http://www.novapublishers.com

All rights reserved. No part of this book may be reproduced, stored in a retrieval system or transmitted in any form or by any means: electronic, electrostatic, magnetic, tape, mechanical photocopying, recording or otherwise without permission from the publishers.

The authors and publisher have taken care in preparation of this book, but make no expressed or implied warranty of any kind and assume no responsibility for any errors or omissions. No liability is assumed for incidental or consequential damages in connection with or arising out of information contained in this book.

This publication is designed to provide accurate and authoritative information with regard to the subject matter covered herein. It is sold with the clear understanding that the publisher is not engaged in rendering legal or any other professional services. If legal or any other expert assistance is required, the services of a competent person should be sought. FROM A DECLARATION OF PARTICIPANTS JOINTLY ADOPTED BY A COMMITTEE OF THE AMERICAN BAR ASSOCIATION AND A COMMITTEE OF PUBLISHERS.

Printed in the United States of America

Contents

Preface		**vii**
Chapter 1	Overview	1
Chapter 2	The Quebec Sovereignty Question	21
Chapter 3	Cuba	25
Chapter 4	U.S. Imports of Canadian Softwood Lumber	29
Chapter 5	U.S.-Canada Steel Trade	33
Chapter 6	Cultural Issues	37
Chapter 7	North American Integration	41
Chapter 8	Canada and the Free Trade Area of the Americas (FTAA)	47
Chapter 9	Canada and the World Trade Organization	51
Chapter 10	Wheat Trade	55
Chapter 11	Dairy Trade	59
Chapter 12	Border Security Issues	65
Chapter 13	Immigration and Refugee Policies	69
Chapter 14	U.S.-Canada Pacific Salmon Management	73
Chapter 15	Waste Issues	77
Chapter 16	Northern Energy Development	81
Index		**87**

PREFACE

During the 1980's, the United States and Canada generally enjoyed very close relations. The early 1990's brought new governments to Ottawa and Washington and although Canada's Liberal Party ran-and won-on a platform that emphasized its intentions to act more independently of the Unites Sates, relations between the two countries have continued to be excellent. The two North American countries continue to cooperate extensively in international security and political issues, both bilaterally and through numerous international organizations. Canada's foreign and defense policies are usually in harmony with those of the United States. Areas of contention are relatively few, but sometimes sharp, as have been the case in the policy towards Cuba. Since September 11, the United States and Canada have cooperated extensively on efforts to combat terrorism. This book provides an overview of Canada's political scene, its economic conditions and its recent security and foreign policy.

Chapter 1

OVERVIEW[1]

The 1980s and early 1990s were marked by an increasingly close U.S.-Canada partnership, whose milestones included the mid-1980s "Shamrock Summits" (named after the Irish heritage shared by the two countries' leaders, Brian Mulroney and Ronald Reagan), the 1988 U.S.-Canada Free Trade Agreement, and the 1993 North American Free Trade Agreement (NAFTA). To many Canadians, however, Ottawa seemed to have drawn a bit *too* close to Washington, D.C., with Canada casting itself too willingly in a secondary role.

In 1994, one Canada watcher observed that in the foreign policy arena, Canada "politely distances itself from the United States" in certain ways.[2] In an interview for a nationally syndicated American magazine, the newly elected Liberal Prime Minister Jean Chrétien summed up his view of the bilateral relationship: "We like each other. I just don't want Canada to be perceived as being the 51st state of America.... With me, a more mature relation will exist between us and the United States."[3]

Some believe, however, that this initial show of mild reserve was intended for domestic consumption — particularly during election campaigns — and that Canada and the United States have in fact continued to enjoy excellent relations. For example, during their first official state meeting, in February 1995, former President Clinton and Prime Minister Chrétien celebrated the signing of a long-discussed "open sides" agreement

---

[1] Prepared by Carl Ek, Specialist in International Relations, Foreign Affairs, Defense, and Trade Division.
[2] Canada Narrows Its Foreign Policy Goals to Focus on Trade. By Charles Trueheart. *Washington Post.* November 17, 1994. p. A44.
[3] Don't Take Canada For Granted. By Tad Szulc. *Parade Magazine.* February 20, 1994. p. 4.

easing restrictions on air travel; the meeting was described as upbeat. The Prime Minister and former President Clinton are said to have had congenial meetings; they focused on areas where the two countries were able to reach agreement, including environmental issues, cooperation on border measures and technology projects.[4]

On February 5, 2001, less than three weeks after his inauguration, President George W. Bush met with Prime Minister Chrétien in Washington. Among other issues, the two leaders reportedly discussed energy, national missile defense, and the April hemispheric trade summit in Quebec City.[5]

Since September 11, however, economic and environmental issues have largely taken backseat to joint efforts to combat international terrorism. On September 24, 2001, Prime Minister Chrétien met in Washington with President Bush. The two discussed possible responses to the attacks on the United States, although President Bush reportedly made no specific requests at that time. Canada became involved in the crisis at the outset – 24 Canadians died in the World Trade Center – and has cooperated closely with the United States in the war on terrorism. In the immediate aftermath of the attacks, U.S. airspace was temporarily closed and Canada allowed more than 200 flights to American destinations to be diverted to Canadian airports.

In the months since the attacks, Canada and the United States have been working together on a number of fronts, including strengthening border security and airline safety, sharing intelligence and expanding law enforcement cooperation. The Canadian government has introduced a new anti-terrorism act, and Canada has contributed significant military assets to the coalition in Afghanistan. President Bush and Prime Minister Chrétien met again in Washington on March 14, 2002; key issues discussed were the softwood lumber dispute, the military campaign in Afghanistan, and the upcoming G-8 summit in Alberta.

CANADIAN DOMESTIC POLITICS

The similarities between the key domestic issues facing the United States and Canada over the past decade have been striking and numerous. At the outset of the 1990s, both governments had big budget deficits to tame, and both were bent upon boosting employment and overhauling their countries' health care and welfare programs. In late 1994, political upheaval

---

[4] Prime Minister Chrétien Visits Washington. *Canada Quarterly*. Vol. 5, Special Issue. April, 1997.
[5] Bush Meets Canadian Leader, By Sonya Ross. AP. February 6, 2001.

beset the two countries as well; after congressional elections, former President Clinton was busy coping with a Republican-controlled Congress, and, after a provincial vote, Chrétien found himself once more face-to-face with the Quebec sovereignty issue. Before the end of their first terms in office, however, both Chrétien and Presidents Clinton and Bush were drawn into international affairs. Crises and entanglements of various kinds abroad have made increasing demands on the attention of North America's leadership.

2000 Elections

Canada's most recent national elections returned a rather fragmented parliament; the 301-member legislature seats five official parties. The three largest parties, which control 276 seats, primarily reflect different and sometimes competing regional interests: the ruling Liberals reign in populous Ontario, in central Canada; the Canadian Alliance, a populist-conservative party that forms the official opposition, hails from the four western Provinces; and the Bloc Québécois is represented only in Quebec.[6] Many observers believe that this polarization of representation complicates the governing process.

Chrétien's party improved its majority by 18 seats in the House of Commons in the 2000 elections. The 36-day campaign was fairly negative by Canadian standards. Over the past five years, speculation has increased in political circles that Chrétien might step down, and that the popular Finance Minister Paul Martin, or one of several other prominent Liberals, may succeed him. Chrétien turned aside a possible challenge during a party convention and declared his intention to serve out his term. Last year, the Liberals deferred their next leadership vote until February 2003, a move observers believe may make for a contentious leadership struggle. Chrétien has made remarks that some believe indicate he intends to remain at the Liberal helm during the next federal elections, which are due by November, 2005 (but may be held earlier).

While the Liberals, with 57% of the seats in parliament, are comfortably situated, the opposition has been weak and fragmented. Repeated attempts to forge closer links between the Canadian Alliance and the Progressive Conservatives – and thereby "unite the right" – have faltered. Stockwell Day, who succeeded Preston Manning as leader of the Canadian Alliance,

---

[6] Canadian parliament's web site: http://www.parl.gc.ca/information/about/processhouse/party standings/standings-e.htm

suffered through a series of missteps, and was replaced in a March, 2002 Alliance leadership vote by fellow Albertan Stephen Harper.

On the provincial level, there have been several leadership changes in the past couple of years: Newfoundland, Saskatchewan, and Quebec (see below) all have new premiers from the same parties as their predecessors. On March 12, 2001, Alberta voters renewed the mandate for the Progressive Conservative party, which has governed the province for 30 years. However, in May 2001 elections, British Columbia voters ousted the scandal-plagued New Democratic Party in favor of a Liberal government; the move, according to some observers, represents a remarkable political swing to the center-right for the province. In Ontario, Tory Premier Mike Harris surprised many in October 2001, when he announced that he would step down; in March, the Conservatives elected former provincial treasurer Ernie Eves to serve out Harris' term.

Economic and Budget Issues

The federal deficit, which stood at a record high C$42 billion when Chrétien became Prime Minister in 1993, was reduced steadily each year.[7] On February 24, 1998, Finance Minister Paul Martin introduced Canada's first balanced budget in nearly three decades. This dramatic elimination of the deficit was accomplished in part through higher man anticipated tax revenues, and through such politically risky measures as cutting back federal funding for health and education transfers, and applying a means test to those who will be eligible for the Seniors Benefit, a newly created entity formed by a merger of the Old Age Security and Guaranteed Income Supplement programs. Many Canadians, long accustomed to their country's extensive system of social programs, objected that the cutbacks created severe hardship for various groups of people, including single parents and the unemployed.

Canadian politicians now find themselves in a post-deficit environment in which they must select among competing demands on annual budget surpluses. Some Canadian officeholders argue that much of the budget surplus should be devoted to large reductions in corporate and income taxes. They maintain that Canada's high taxation, relative to that of other countries, discourages job creation, reduces household incomes, diminishes worker productivity, and causes a "brain drain" of Canadian professionals, chiefly to

---

[7] As of May 1, 2002, one Canadian dollar equals US$0.6398.

the United States. However, other policymakers point out that Canada's current tax system enables the government to maintain a host of social programs that make Canada the envy of many countries; in addition, they note that, high taxes notwithstanding, thousands of talented people emigrate to Canada every year.[8]

Responding to calls for lower taxes, for measures that would stimulate the economy, and for greater resources for social programs and national security, the government unveiled in December 2001 a budget that emphasized tax cuts, emergency preparedness and other security-related areas, and health care and early childhood development programs.[9]

National Unity

For nearly four decades, an emotional debate has raged over the status of French-speaking Quebec, Canada's largest province and home to 25% of its population. Many Québécois are concerned that their language and culture will be overwhelmed by the rest of English-speaking Canada. Some believe that their society may only be preserved if Quebec separates from the rest of Canada and forms an independent country.

In October 1994 elections, after the Liberals had governed Quebec for several years, the province once more elected the separatist Parti Québécois (PQ). The victorious PQ held a referendum on sovereignty on October 30,1995. Quebeckers voted on whether they wished to continue to remain a part of Canada, or strike off on their own. The question was decided by the narrowest of margins — the vote went 50.6 percent to 49.4 percent in favor of keeping the country whole. The wafer-thin margin shocked federalists and separatists alike. The country is still affected by the impact of what has been called a "near-death experience," and both sides have continued politicking in anticipation of a possible third referendum.[10]

Quebec held provincial elections once again in October 1998. Although the Liberals won a slight plurality of the total votes, their support was concentrated in and around Montreal, and the PQ retained a comfortable majority in the provincial legislature. Lucien Bouchard, the charismatic premier, subsequently announced that he would not call another referendum

---

[8] See: The Tax Trap. By Mary Janigan. *Maclean's*. April 12, 1999. p. 14. And: The Brain Drain: Myth and Reality, By Ross Finnic, *Choices*. Vol. 7, No. 6. November 2001.
[9] Budget 2001 Builds On Long-term Plan and Responds To Immediate Personal and Economic Security Concerns. News Release. Department of Finance Canada. December 10, 2001, http://www.fin.gc.ca/news01/01-118e.html
[10] A 1980 referendum on "sovereignty-association" for Quebec was defeated 60%-40%.

until "winning conditions" were evident. A poll in mid-December 1999 indicated that just 30% of Quebeckers would vote for independence;[11] nevertheless, Premier Bouchard pledged a renewed push for sovereignty. Then, in January 2001, Bouchard stunned the province and the nation by announcing that he would resign his post. His successor, Bernard Landry, is regarded as a hard-line sovereigntist. In a recent speech, Landry indicated he would hold another referendum after the next provincial elections, which must be held by November 2003. On April 15, however, the PQ lost three provincial by-elections; observers believe that, although Landry personally is popular in the province, the Pequists are trailing the Liberals in popularity and might not prevail in the next election.[12] Canada's time of political turmoil will likely continue as it seeks to resolve the Quebec issue.[13]

U.S. Position

U.S. policymakers will continue to watch developments on this issue with interest. Since the debate began in the 1960s, the United States government has assiduously sought to remain officially neutral on the issue of Quebec, continually repeating the three-point "mantra" that the United States enjoys excellent relations with a strong and united Canada; that the Quebec question is an internal issue that is for Canadians to decide; and that the United States does not wish to interfere with Canada's domestic matters. However, some analysts detected a slight "tilt" on the part of Clinton Administration toward the federalists during the 1995 referendum campaign. During a 1998 visit to Ottawa, former Secretary of State Albright delivered remarks — in English and French — that, in the opinion of some observers, reinforced the perception that U.S. policy favored a united Canada. And during a 1999 visit to Canada, former President Clinton declared that the United States valued its relations with "a strong, united and democratic Canada." If, in the future, Quebec eventually *does* leave the confederation, the U.S. government will be faced with difficult political and economic questions.[14]

---

[11] Separatism Near Extinction: Poll. By Campbell Clark and Robert Fife. *The National Post.* December 15, 1999.
[12] Referendum Still PQ Priority. By Aaron Derfel. *Montreal Gazette.* April 15, 2002. Landry Vows to Stay Despite Losses at Polls. By Allison Hanes. *National Post.* April 17,2002. p.A06.
[13] For additional background on the unity issue, see: Canada's Coup D'éclat. By Christopher Sands. *CSIS Hemisphere 2000.* Series VIII, Issue 6. March 27, 2000.
[14] Albright Says U.S. Prefers United Canada. *Ottawa Citizen.* March 11, 1998. President Clinton Meets with Chrétien, Opens New U.S. Embassy. *Canada Quarterly.* October, 1999. The

SECURITY AND FOREIGN POLICY ISSUES

Security Isses

The degree and manner in which Canada's budget austerity has affected its military forces and their involvement in foreign security operations are matters of great interest to U.S. policymakers. According to the U.S. State Department, "U.S. defense arrangements with Canada are more extensive than with any other country."[15]

Over the past century, U.S.-Canadian defense cooperation has been close; during peacetime, it has occurred chiefly in the context of multinational organizations. Since the United Nations first dispatched an armed peacekeeping contingent — to help defuse the Suez Crisis in 1956 — Canada has participated in nearly every U.N. peacekeeping operation, from Cyprus and the Sinai, to Bosnia, Rwanda and Somalia; Canadians are proud of their active role as peacekeepers. As of May 2002, there were 4,139 Canadian forces participating in international operations in Afghanistan, the Balkans, the Middle East, and Africa.[16]

As with other countries in the 1990s, Canada's military was subject to dual pressures. In Ottawa's view, the collapse of the Soviet Union and the Warsaw Pact reduced the military threat, making it more difficult for the government to justify sustaining historic spending levels on defense. Leaders believed that the country's large debt early in the decade necessitated funding cutbacks in most areas of government, including defense. However, relative to its NATO allies, Canada had been devoting only a modest share — about 2% of GDP — of its budget to defense spending over the past two decades (including the Cold War). That percentage declined further, from 2.01% in 1990 to 1.2% in 2000 — among NATO members, only Luxembourg and Iceland (which has no armed forces) spend a lower percentage. Canada's modest military budget has irked some within the alliance. During a November 2000 visit to Ottawa, NATO Secretary-General

---

Quebec Sovereignty Question, by Carl W. Ek and Stephen F. Clarke. CRS Report 94-886 F. November 16, 1994. Quebec's 1995 Referendum and Future Prospects, by Carl W. Ek and Stephen F. Clarke. CRS Report 96-3 F. December 19, 1995.

[15] United States Department of State. Bureau of Western Hemisphere Affairs. *Background Note: Canada.* June, 2001.

[16] Canada and International Peacekeeping. By Joseph T. Jockel. Center for Strategic and International Studies/Canadian Institute of Strategic Studies. Washington, D.C., and Toronto, Ontario. 1994. CF Operations Week Ahead 04 May-10 May 2002. Canadian DND web page: http://www.dnd.ca/menu/operations/index_e.htm

Lord George Robertson publicly chided Canada for spending about half of the NATO average on defense.[17]

After the round of cutbacks in the 1990s, the number of active personnel in Canada's armed forces tumbled more than 15%, to 56,800 in late 2001.[18] The Canadian forces are also strapped for resources to replace aging equipment. This trend has disturbed many in the military, and, along with other factors, may be affecting morale. In February 1996, the Canadian Chief of Defence Staff stated that his troops would be unprepared for "high intensity" combat.[19] More than two years later, Canada's Auditor General cautioned that an equipment budget shortfall might result in "reduced capabilities."[20] Some analysts have charged that continued low levels of defense spending may hamper Canada's international reputation through creating a "commitment-capability gap."[21] A Canadian editorialist recently declared that "[w]e have effectively signed over responsibility for our national defence to the United States by allowing our own military to become so diminished in size and the quality of its equipment."[22]

In December 2001, the government announced that an additional C$1.6 billion would be spent over the next 5 years on defense-related activities, including improving anti-terrorism capabilities.[23] Defense Minister Art Eggleton has argued that, since he took office in 1997, Canada's military budget has increased from C$9.8 billion to C$12.5 billion. On February 22, 2002, Eggleton announced that, in view of the changed security environment, his department would conduct a thorough review of Canadian defense policy that would examine all facets of the military, from capabilities to costs to force structure. The last such defense policy overhaul

---

[17] Canadian Defense Policy and the Future of Canada-United States Security Relations. By Joel J. Sokolsky and David Detomasi. *The American Review of Canadian Studies (ARCS)*. No. 4. Winter, 1994. p. 537. U.S. Department of Defense. *Report on Allied Contributions to the Common Defense: A Report to the United States Congress by the Secretary of Defense.* March, 2001. http://www.defenselink.mil/pubs/allied_contrib2001/allied2001.pdf NATO Head Hits Canada on Defence Spending. By Jeff Sallot. *The Globe and Mail.* November 4, 1999.

[18] *The Military Balance, 2001/2002.* Oxford Univ. Press. London. October 2001. p. 49.

[19] A Shot Across the Bow: The Chief Says His Forces are Unfit for War. By Luke Fisher. *Maclean's.* February 26, 1996. p. 25.

[20] Canadian Military Anticipates No Help for Budget Shortfall. By David Pugliese. *Defense News.* May 4-10, 1998. p. 10.

[21] Military Criticized for Rhetoric on Peace: Canada Accused of 'Speaking Loudly and Carrying a Bent Twig.' By Mike Blanchfield. *Ottawa Citizen.* March 23, 2001. p. Al.

[22] Afghanistan in the Wake of Death. By Anthony Wilson-Smith. *Maclean's.* April 29, 2002. Vol. 115, No. 17. p.2.

[23] For highlights of the 2001 budget, see the Canadian Department of National Defence web site: http://www.dnd.ca/menu/budget01/highlight_e.htm

took place in 1994. Eggleton aims to have the review complete by the fall of 2003.

On March 2, the Canadian Senate's Committee on National Security and Defence released a report calling for the government to increase defense spending by $4 billion to counter the threat of international terrorism. Among other steps, the report recommends that military personnel levels be increased by 20,000 and that additional resources be provided to the Canadian Security Intelligence Service. The report also called for an inquiry into possible linkages between extremist groups and organized crime activities in Canadian ports.[24]

U.S.-Canada Security Issues

Canada and the United States cooperate actively in the defense arena. In June 2000, Canada and the United States agreed to renew the 43-year old North American Aerospace Defense Command (NORAD) agreement. The continental air defense pact, which monitors U.S. and Canadian airspace, called for joint efforts in aerospace technologies; its five-year renewal took effect in May 2001. In the wake of the September 11 terrorist attacks, there have been discussions of deepening military cooperation along the NORAD model – in the context of the Bush Administration's newly-proposed Northern Command – to include land and sea forces; some Canadians, however, are concerned that such a move might impinge upon Canada's sovereignty.[25] Finally, in February 2002 Canada agreed to participate in the further development of the U.S.-led Joint Strike Fighter program, contributing $150 million over a 10-year period.

Although it has no troops stationed in NATO territory in Europe, Canada currently is contributing about 1,500 troops to the NATO-led Stabilization Force (SFOR) deployed to police the truce in Bosnia, 10 support personnel in the peacekeeping mission in Kosovo (KFOR), as well as over 200 observers with UN operations in the Middle East and Africa.[26]

---

[24] Canada's Security at Risk. By Jim Bronskill. *Ottawa Citizen.* March 2, 2002. p. A2.
[25] Continental Divides. By Sydney J. Freedberg, *Jr. National Journal.* March 23, 2002. See also: Leading academics Examine Risks Inherent in Closer Military Co-operation with the United States. Canada News Wire. April 26, 2002.
[26] Kosovo and Macedonia: U.S. and Allied Military Operations, by Steven R. Bowman. CRS Issue Brief IB10027. Updated periodically. Bosnia: U.S. Military Operations, by Steven R. Bowman. CRS Issue Brief IB93056. Updated periodically. Canadian Department of National Defence. United Nations Peace Support Operations Update. March, 2002, http://www.dnd.ca/admpol/org/dg_is/d_pk/sitrep_mar02_e.htm

Canada also supplied 200 troops to NATO's mission in Macedonia, and 600 to the initial UN peacekeeping mission in East Timor.

Canada is also engaged in the debate over NATO's future. At the July 8, 1997 NATO summit in Madrid, Canada sided with eight European member states that favored the expansion of the alliance by five countries, rather than three, as urged by the United States; the U.S. position prevailed. In January 1998, Canada became the first NATO member to ratify enlargement to include Poland, the Czech Republic, and Hungary – which formally entered the alliance on March 12, 1999. Canada believes that several of the countries currently aspiring to join NATO have fulfilled their reform requirements, and that their membership would enhance transatlantic security; Ottawa therefore supports a "broader" enlargement at the Prague Summit in November 2002. In addition, Ottawa and Brussels recently have been negotiating the issue of Canadian participation in NATO/EU crisis management operations that might be undertaken by the European Union's nascent rapid reaction force.[27]

Ottawa also has been debating the U.S. proposal to deploy a National Missile Defense (NMD) system. Former Foreign Affairs Minister Loyd Axworthy expressed reservations over the planned NMD, in the belief that it might spark a new arms race, while Defense Minister Art Eggleton reportedly would like to keep Canada's options open on the subject, perhaps with a view toward incorporating an eventual missile defense system into NORAD. Parliament has held hearings on the issue, but no official policy has yet been enunciated. After a February 2001 meeting between Bush and Chrétien, however, the *Toronto Globe and Mail* noted that "Ottawa has subtly shifted its rhetoric on President George W. Bush's controversial antimissile defence shield, from echoing the Kremlin's objections to stressing close continental military co-operation."[28] In May 2001, the *National Post,* quoting an unnamed senior government official, reported that the government had determined that it would back NMD "in the end;" however, spokespersons for the Defense and Foreign Ministers disavowed that statement.[29] Finally, the Canadian government has repeatedly stated its opposition to the "weaponization" of space.

---

[27] Canada Near Deal to Join EU Rapid Force. Andrew McIntosh and Michael Petrou. *National Post.* May 4, 2002. p. A01. See also: NATO: Issues for Congress, by Paul E. Gallis. CRS Report RL 31109. August 31, 2001.

[28] Canada Wants Time to Consider Participation in U.S. NMD System. By Michael Sirak. *Inside Missile Defense.* April 19, 2000. p. 1. PM Changes Tone on Missile Shield. By PaulKoring. *Toronto Globe and Mail.* February 8, 2001.

[29] Canada to Back Missile Shield. By Robert Fife. *The National Post.* May 14, 2001. Canada Rejects Report It Will Join U.S. Arms Plan. Reuters. May 14, 2001.

Budget cuts notwithstanding, Canada cooperated "wing-to-wing" with the United States in *Operation Allied Force,* the NATO campaign of airstrikes against targets in Serbia and Kosovo. Canada contributed eighteen CF-18 fighter aircraft, and provided two rotations of approximately 1500 troops each to KFOR.

Canada has also made military contributions to the war on terrorism. In October, 2001 the government launched *Operation Apollo,* in support of U.S. *Operation Enduring Freedom.* Currently, there are 880 light infantry troops of the 3rd Battalion Princess Patricia's Canadian Light Infantry Battle Group and approximately 40 members of Canada's special forces unit – Joint Task Force 2 – serving in Afghanistan. The Canadians' main task has been to assist the U.S. 101st Airborne in providing security at the air base at Kandahar, but they have also been involved in delivering humanitarian aid, and in combat missions – including *Operation Anaconda* – to root out remaining elements of the Taliban and Al Qaeda. Other Canadian military assets supporting Operation Enduring Freedom include a naval task group, consisting of 4 frigates, a destroyer, and a replenishment ship, all serving in the Arabian Sea, and a half-dozen transport and surveillance aircraft.[30]

On April 18, 2002, while their unit was conducting live fire exercises near Kandahar, Afghanistan, four Canadian soldiers were killed and eight others wounded when a bomb dropped by an American F-16 fighter struck their position. They were the first combat deaths for Canada since the Korean War. Both the White House and Congress have expressed condolences and sorrow over the tragic accident, and a joint investigation is underway.

Foreign Policy Issues

Some analysts concluded that, after first taking office, Chrétien had "tilted Canada's foreign policy towards the more explicit pursuit of economic self-interest and away from concerns about human rights abroad."[31] Under Lloyd Axworthy's leadership beginning in 1996, however, many observers detected a swing in attitude at the Foreign Affairs Ministry back toward Canada assuming the role of "soft power," relying on its

---

[30] See: The Canadian Forces Contribution to the International Campaign Against Terrorism. http://www.dnd.ca/eng/archive/2002/mar02/7/mar02_b_e.htm. For a summary of forces in Operation Apollo, see: http://www.dnd.ca/menu/operation/Apollo/index_e.htm.
[31] Canada Bows out as "Boy Scout" to the World. By Jeffrey Simpson. *Hemisfile: Perspectives on Political and Economic Trends in the America.* July/August, 1995. p. 4.

reputation as an honest broker to help effect consensus through negotiation and moral suasion rather than military force or economic sanctions.[32] In the most significant example of this approach, Axworthy launched the "Ottawa process" to reach agreement on a treaty banning the manufacture, trade, and use of antipersonnel land mines; the effort culminated in a December 1997 conference at which more than 100 nations signed the accord. Axworthy also sought to launch a similar international ban on small arms, and attempted to generate interest among other countries in promoting an international "humanitarian agenda."[33] The United States did not sign the pact.

John Manley replaced Axworthy in 2000. In January 2002, after a major cabinet reshuffle by Chrétien, Manley became Deputy Prime Minister and Bill Graham, chairman of the parliamentary committee on foreign affairs and international trade, was named Minister of Foreign Affairs. According to one writer, Graham "can often sound like Axworthy."[34] Others, however, believe Graham may place more emphasis on pragmatism; early in his tenure, he launched a foreign policy review process.

As a middle power, Canada has exercised a somewhat disproportionate influence in world affairs, chiefly through its active participation in international organizations, including the G-8, and the Asia-Pacific Economic Cooperation forum. In 1998, Canadian diplomat Louise Frechette was named Deputy Secretary General of the United Nations, and a year later, Canada was voted one of the 10 rotating, 2-year seats on the U.N. Security Council. Also, the Organization for Economic Cooperation and Development (OECD) is led by a Canadian (former cabinet minister Donald Johnston), and the first head of the U.N. War Crimes Tribunal was Canadian Louise Arbour. In April 2001, Quebec City was the site of the third Summit of the Americas, attended by 34 heads of state, and in 2002, Canada will once more host the G-8 summit.

Canada and the United States have worked closely together in a number of troubled regions. One example of such cooperation is the U.N. mission in Haiti, where a contingent of the Canadian armed forces, along with members of the Royal Canadian Mounted Police, took the reins from the departing U.S. forces who helped restore the democratically elected government in

---

[32] Canada to Play Global Role as 'Soft Power.' By Mike Trickey. *Ottawa Citizen.* March 3, 1998. p. A5. For a critical view, see: Ottawa's New-Age Diplomacy Ruffles Many Feathers in Washington. By Steven Pearlstein. *International Herald Tribune.* February 22, 1999. p. 3.

[33] See: Canadian Department of Foreign Affairs and International Trade. Human Security: Safety for People in a Changing World. Ottawa. April, 1999.

[34] Out of Africa: The Perils For A PM. By Anthony Wilson-Smith. *Maclean's.* March 25, 2002. p. 4.

Haiti. Gen. John de Chastelain, former chief of Canada's defense staff, served under former U.S. Senator George Mitchell to chair parts of the Northern Ireland peace talks; the talks led to the historic political settlement announced on April 10, 1998.

At the upcoming G-8 meeting, which will be held in June 2002 in Kananaskis, Alberta, representatives will discuss, among other issues, the New Partnership for Africa's Development, a plan drafted by Africans to improve the continent's governance, trade, and economic development. Several African leaders have been invited to the summit.

U.S.-Canada Agenda

During the 1998 standoff with Iraq, Canada, although skeptical at first, eventually sided with the United States on the use of military force against Saddam Hussein if diplomacy failed to achieve unrestricted access for inspections for weapons of mass destruction. However, Canada currently appears to be disinclined to expand the war on terrorism beyond Afghanistan to Iraq. In February 2002, during a visit with Chrétien to Moscow, Foreign Affairs Minister Graham stated that Canada would oppose U.S. unilateral action against Iraq unless Baghdad were linked to terrorism, or it were "shown that they are amassing their weapons of mass destruction with a vision of using them against someone in the immediate future...." One month later, when asked by a journalist whether Canada would require "tangible proof of a connection between terrorists and the Iraqi government before Canada would consider joining a military action against Iraq, Graham replied "Yes, absolutely."[35]

Cuba, however, is another area of foreign policy where the two countries do not see eye-to-eye. For decades, Canada and Cuba have enjoyed relatively extensive business links. Because of this ongoing commercial relationship, Canadian government officials have publicly criticized U.S. legislation (the Cuban Liberty and Democratic Solidarity Act, P.L. 104-114) that seeks to apply indirect pressure on the Castro regime by permitting Cuban-Americans to file lawsuits against foreign firms that utilize Cuban property that was expropriated by the Castro regime. However, the President is permitted to waive this provision under certain conditions for six-month periods. The law may also restrict entry into the United States of officers,

---

[35] Canada Won't Back War on Iraq. By Mike Trickey and Hilary Mackenzie. *Ottawa Citizen*. February 15, 2002. p. A1. Canada FM Requires Proof of Terror Links for War Beyond Afghanistan. *AFP*. March 11, 2002.

principals, or shareholders of such firms, along with their close relatives; to date, several executives of Sherritt International, a Canadian mining company, have been banned from entry into the United States. U. S. supporters of the Cuba embargo have been critical of Canadian mining companies and hotel chains that do business with the island nation. Canadians, who are sensitive to being perceived as America's "junior partner," object that the law amounts to the United States forcing its foreign and commercial policies upon other countries.

In April 1998, after attending the Summit of the Americas meeting in Santiago, Chile, Chrétien stopped over in Cuba; while there, he publically urged Castro to release several political prisoners. After the visit, the Prime Minister told reporters "I think he [Castro] is changing."[36] One year later, however, four prominent Cuban dissidents received harsh prison sentences, and Ottawa has undertaken a review of its policies toward Havana. Canadian officials have characterized the relationship recently as cool. Citing Cuba's lack of democracy, Canada chose not to invite Cuba to the 2001 Summit of the Americas in Quebec City.

The most recent incident relating to Cuba occurred on April 3, 2002, when a Canadian businessman – and U.S. resident – was convicted by a U.S. federal court of violating the U. S. trade embargo. Several Canadian Members of Parliament have objected to the court ruling, arguing that it constitutes an affront to Canadian sovereignty.

The International Criminal Court (ICC) is another issue on which the two countries differ. Canada has long been a leading advocate of the UN-sponsored tribunal, while some U.S. policymakers have opposed U.S. participation on the grounds that it might make U.S. military personnel vulnerable to politically motivated prosecution by hostile regimes. On May 6, 2002, the Bush Administration declared that the United States would not support the ICC; in an interview the same day, Canadian Foreign Affairs Minister Graham declared that he was "extremely disappointed" with the U.S. decision.[37]

In the wake of the attacks on New York and Washington, U.S.-Canadian relations came to the fore. In particular, the issue of U.S.-Canada border security was brought into sharp focus. The issue first became a matter of urgent concern in December 1999, when suspected terrorist Ahmed Ressam was stopped at the U.S.-Canadian border attempting to smuggle explosives

---

[36] Jean and Fidel: How a Pragmatist Tried to Sway an Ideologue. By Brace Wallace. *Maclean's*. May 11, 1998. p. 28.

[37] Canada Raps U.S. Rejection Of World Criminal Court. By David Ljunggren. *Reuters*. May 6, 2002.

into the United States; it was later discovered that Ressam had planned to bomb the Los Angeles airport, and that he had received terrorist training from Al-Qaeda in Afghanistan. Despite the fact that none of the 19 September 11 highjackers entered from Canada, the attacks sparked renewed debate over Canadian laws regarding the treatment of immigrants seeking refugee status or political asylum.[38] According to one report, Ottawa is already "taking steps to tighten immigration and refugee policies, including more rigorous screening of people who claim refugee status and stepped up detentions and deportations of claimants suspected of being security risks."[39] In addition, the two countries have been coordinating visa policies.

Some American policymakers pointed to the Ressam case as proof that the United States must tighten its borders with Canada. Skeptics, however, note that such measures might seriously impede commerce by creating long delays at border crossings, and that terrorists and criminals would at best be inconvenienced, not stopped, in traversing the two countries' 5500-mile border. Since September, Ottawa and Washington, have taken numerous steps – separately and jointly – to improve border control.[40] In December 2001, they signed two agreements (the Smart Border declaration, and the Joint Statement on Cooperation on Border Security and Regional Migration Issues) that aim at improving security and efficiency at border crossings. Canada's custom service has stepped up the purchase of high-tech X-ray equipment, and U.S. Customs agents have been invited to work at three major Canadian seaports. Border security personnel levels have also been beefed up. Canada has established an Air Transport Security Authority, which, among other activities, will be responsible for pre-board screening.

Finally, Canada has taken other actions beyond the realm of border security, including freezing terrorists' assets, broadening the scope of terrorist activities punishable by law, extending police investigative powers, introducing legislation that would put restraints on fund-raising activities by extremist organizations, expanding cooperation between the FBI and the Royal Canadian Mounted Police, and increasing outlays for Canada's intelligence service and for countering nuclear, biological, and chemical weapons attacks.

---

[38] Al-Qaida in Canada? CBSNEWS.com. April 25, 2002.
[39] Canada Alters Security Policy to Ease Concerns of U.S. By Clifford Krauss. *New York Times*. February 18, 2002.
[40] See: Backgrounder: Canada's Actions Against Terrorism Since September 11. Department of Foreign Affairs and International Trade web page (updated April 18, 2002). http://www.dfait-maeci.gc.ca/anti-terrorism/canadaactions-e.asp.

ECONOMIC AND TRADE ISSUES

Prime Minister Chrétien ran in 1993 on a platform that emphasized putting Canadians back to work and stimulating growth in the economy, which had suffered from a three-year recession. Since the October 1993 elections, the unemployment figure has sunk five percentage points, to 6.8% in 2001; by March 2002, joblessness had risen to 7.7%. After rather lackluster post-recession growth rates of 2.3% in 1995 and 1.5% in 1996, Canada's GDP rose a robust 4.4% in 1997, 3.3% in 1998, 4.5% in 1999, and 4.4% in 2000. Growth in 2001 was just 1.5%; the decline was attributed in part to the economic slowdown in the United States; a somewhat higher growth rate is forecast for 2002. In March 2002, inflation stood at 1.8%.[41]

Although the Canadian economy overall is in healthy condition, the prosperity has been somewhat uneven, particularly in the west. British Columbia suffered from Asia's financial turmoil, and the prairie provinces from depressed grain and livestock markets. In addition, the value of the Canadian dollar (known as the "loonie") in 1998 declined dramatically vis-a-vis the U.S. dollar and other major currencies; although this helps the export sector somewhat, Canadian tourists make millions of trips to the United States and other countries each year, and those visits are now much less affordable.

In the 1990s, Canada's export sector increasingly accounted for a significant share of the economy. Overseas sales soared in 1994 but stalled somewhat in 1995; Canadian analysts attributed this to a slowdown among Canada's trading partners. However, in 2001, Canada had a C$29.1 billion current account surplus with the world. Many Canadians are encouraged by the recent recovery from recession of the United States, by far the largest foreign market for Canadian goods.

In keeping with his party's stated goal of increasing and diversifying overseas markets, Chrétien has employed a "Team Canada" approach; between April 1998 and May 2000, there have been 8 Team Canada missions to Europe, Africa, Asia, and the United States. In February 2001, the Team returned to China, and one year later, Chrétien accompanied a 300-member Team went to Russia and Germany. In addition, Canada has been pursuing a free trade pact with the 4-member European Free Trade Association.

---

[41] Economic data are from: Economist Intelligence Unit. April, 2002. Finance Canada. The Economy in Brief 2002. March, 2002. http://www.fin.gc.ca/ECONBR/ecbr02-03e.html Statistics Canada: http://www.statcan.ca/start.html.

Bilateral Trade Issues

The United States and Canada enjoy the largest bilateral commercial relationship in the world; the U.S. State Department estimated total two-way trade in 2001 at $1.4 billion *per day*.[42] Many analysts believe that the sharp differences of the past – over diverse items ranging from automobiles to peanut butter – are not as prominent today. A likely reason for this is the conclusion of two important bilateral treaties: the 1988 U.S. Canada Free Trade Agreement and the 1993 North American Free Trade Agreement.[43] These documents, along with major revisions in the Uruguay Round of the General Agreement on Tariffs and Trade and the creation of the World Trade Organization (WTO), contained mutual concessions on commercial trade barriers, and, more importantly perhaps, established – or improved upon – mechanisms for resolving disputes.[44]

Nevertheless, several trade issues – some old, some new – have yet to be completely resolved. Many of these disputes involve long-running battles over agricultural commodities or natural resources, including softwood lumber, grains, and dairy and poultry products. Some analysts attribute the longevity of these conflicts to the inherent incompatibility of the two countries' different natural resource and agricultural programs, others to the political sensitivity of the commodities under negotiation.

A more recent group of complaints, categorized by Canadian policy makers as "cultural industries," and by their American counterparts as "entertainment industries," has roused emotions on both sides of the border. Canadians, aware that their population is only one-tenth that of the United States, are anxious that their society is being increasingly Americanized over the airwaves, on cinema screens, and at the newsstands. They have sought to block this trend on several fronts: by prohibiting "split issues" (foreign content and Canadian advertising) of *Sports Illustrated magazine,* by canceling the license of a U.S. country music station, and by denying entry to large U.S. bookstore chains. The United States has vigorously objected to these moves, arguing that they are motivated more by economic than by cultural interests, and that the principle of free trade should apply to the entertainment industry as well as to other goods and services. In May 1999, Canada and the United States reached an agreement under which American

---

[42] U.S. Department of State. Bureau of Western Hemisphere Affairs. Background Note: Canada. June 2001. http://www.state.gov/r/pa/ei/bgn/2089pf.htm

[43] See: CRS Report 97-889, *NAFTA's Effects on Canada-U.S. Trade and Investment,* by Arlene Wilson. November 27, 1997.

publications will be allowed gradual access to the Canadian market. In return, the United States agreed not to take action against Canada unilaterally or through the WTO or FTA.

Regardless of the occasional rancor of U.S.-Canadian trade disputes, there is little danger that such conflicts would ever escalate into a full-blown trade war. The Canadians in particular have a strong incentive to resolve feuds and maintain close trade ties with the United States. The Canadian economy is heavily export-oriented, and its largest trading partner by far is the United States, which last year took 86% of Canada's exports and was the source of about three-quarters of its imports. And although sharp disputes still plague the enormous bilateral trade relationship, it is important to keep in mind that "normally no more than 1 to 2 percent of each country's merchandise exports are under investigation in any year."[45]

ENVIRONMENTAL ISSUES

The United States and Canada, which share a common border that stretches 5,500 miles, cooperate extensively on environmental matters. Since they signed the Boundary Waters Treaty in 1909, the two countries have, through the International Joint Commission, worked together on protecting and maintaining border waterways — especially the Great Lakes. In 1978, the two signed the Great Lakes Water Quality Agreement.

The long feud over Pacific salmon — perhaps the most prominent bilateral dispute in recent years — had both environmental and commercial aspects. Canada contended that American fishermen were taking more than their equitable share of the migratory fish; the United States, on the other hand, maintained that its fishing was in accordance with the 1985 Pacific Salmon Treaty and with sound conservation practices. Talks resumed in 1997, and the two sides finally reached an accord in 1999; both countries are monitoring implementation of the agreement.[46]

Other environmental problems the two countries have dealt with in recent years include secondary wastewater treatment, control of predator fish introduced into the Lakes by ocean-going vessels, and sustainability of the

---

[44] See: Current State of U.S.-Canada Economic Relations. By Sidney Weintraub. In *ARCS,* p. 473.
[45] Canada-U.S. Relations on the Eve of President Clinton's State Visit to Canada. By Sidney Weintraub and Chris Sands. *CSIS Policy Papers on the Americas.* Vol. VI, Report I. February 17, 1995. p. 5.
[46] The Pacific Salmon Treaty: The 1999 Agreement in Historical Perspective, by Daniel A. Waldeck and Eugene H. Buck. CRS Report RL30234. Updated Oct. 18, 1999.

St. Lawrence Seaway. In addition, the United States and Canada concluded a hazardous waste trade agreement in 1986; more recently, transboundary shipments of solid waste, particularly from Ontario to Ohio, Michigan, and several other states, have been under review. The two countries have continued the long-standing debate over the ecological impact of possible development in Alaska's Arctic National Wildlife Refuge. Finally, the two sides continue to monitor the progress of the 1991 Canada-United States Air Quality Agreement.

Chapter 2

THE QUEBEC SOVEREIGNTY QUESTION[1]

ISSUE DEFINITION

On October 30, 1995, residents of Canada's French-speaking province of Quebec held a referendum on whether they wished to continue to remain a part of Canada or form an independent country. Unity supporters prevailed, but just barely; the final tally was 50.6%-49.4%. Canada is still seeking to resolve the Quebec question. U.S. policymakers are watching this process with interest. If, in the future, Quebec eventually *does* leave the confederation, the U.S. government will be faced with difficult political and economic questions.

BACKGROUND AND ANALYSIS

Over the past four decades, an emotional debate has raged in Canada over the status of French-speaking Quebec, the country's largest province and home to 25% of its population. Many Québécois are concerned that their language and culture will be lost through assimilation with the rest of English-speaking Canada; some assert that their Francophone society can only be preserved if Quebec separates from the rest of Canada and forms an independent country.

Some observers believe that Quebec nationalism began to intensify once more after a 1980 referendum on "sovereignty association" was defeated 40% to 60%. Quebec leaders have asserted that their province was

---

[1] Prepared by Carl Ek, Specialist in International Relations, CRS Foreign Affairs, Defense, and Trade Division.

humiliated in 1982, when the federal government and the nine other provinces agreed to "patriate" Canada's Constitution from Great Britain without the concurrence of Quebec's National Assembly. Many hoped that subsequent constitutional reforms would reassure Quebec, but two agreements (the Meech Lake and Charlottetown accords) that would have, *inter alia,* recognized Quebec as a "distinct society," failed to be approved.

In 1990, following the collapse of the first of these accords, the separatist Bloc Québécois (BQ) was formed; in the 1993 general elections, it won the second largest number of seats in Parliament and was, for four years, the opposition party. In 1994, the BQ's provincial counterpart, the Parti Québécois (PQ), won the provincial elections in Quebec; the PQ held the referendum one year later, and nearly prevailed. Both sides have been politicking in anticipation of a possible third plebiscite.

Successive U.S. administrations have publicly maintained a neutral position on the Quebec issue, although some observers noted a distinct tilt toward the federalist side during the last referendum. The official position is that the United States enjoys excellent relations with a strong and united Canada; that the Quebec question is an internal issue that is for Canadians to decide; and that the United States does not wish to interfere with Canada's domestic matters.

STATUS OF THE ISSUE

Since the referendum, the Chrétien administration has set for itself the difficult task of addressing the objections of Quebec separatists without aggravating Canadians in the other provinces, especially in the west. Shortly after the vote, the Prime Minister announced proposals that signaled Chrétien's determination to seek a unity compromise. In September 1997, following a conference in Alberta, nine provincial premiers issued the "Calgary declaration," a seven-point framework for national discussion. The document acknowledged the "unique character" of Quebec, but added that all provinces have "equality of status."

Surveys have indicated that many Quebeckers are dissatisfied with the status quo, but do not favor separation; it is this group that Chrétien and others are seeking to accommodate. The government has been reviewing existing federal authorities to determine whether provincial governments could be more effective; Ottawa has also relaxed conditions placed on programs it funds in the provinces. Such changes are welcome not only in Quebec, but in other provinces as well.

In 1996, the federal government contested the constitutionality and international legality of a province making a "unilateral declaration of independence." In August 1998, the Supreme Court ruled that the constitution did not provide for unilateral secession, but that if a provincial referendum indicated that a clear majority favored independence, negotiations addressing the interests of all provinces, the federal government, and minorities, should follow.

Many federalists argue that if Quebec ever does vote to secede, the rest of Canada should have a say in the decision and, if it agrees to a split, to the terms of separation. Unity supporters have been debating a number of proposals aimed at defining the circumstances under which Ottawa might approve a Quebec bid to leave the federation. These focus upon establishing certain guarantees; among them, that Quebeckers would vote on a clear, yes/no question. In March 2000, the Commons passed the Clarity Bill, which would grant parliament authority to determine whether or not any future referendum were be based upon Quebeckers' responses to a clear-cut question. In addition, Canadians have been discussing a concept called "partitioning," which says that if Canada is divisible, then so is Quebec — in the event of a split, a large chunk of the northern part of the province, inhabited mainly by native Canadians, would remain a part of Canada, as would parts of non-French-speaking Montreal. Sovereigntists adamantly reject this notion.

Quebec held its most recent provincial elections in the fall of 1998 and the PQ retained its majority in the legislature. Premier Lucien Bouchard subsequently announced that he would not call another referendum until "winning conditions" were evident. At a PQ convention in early May 2000, however, Bouchard pledged a renewed push for sovereignty. In January 2001, Bouchard stunned the province and the nation by announcing that he would resign. His successor, Bernard Landry, is regarded as a hard-line sovereigntist. In a recent speech, Landry indicated he would hold another referendum after the next provincial elections, which must be held by November 2003. On April 15, 2002, however, the PQ lost three provincial by-elections; observers believe the Pequists are trailing the Liberals in popularity.

QUESTIONS

1. How might Americans regard and respond to the possible creation of an independent Quebec? What are the potential effects and changes on

current U.S.-Canada trade relations (especially in the context of NAFTA), environmental cooperation, and political and security arrangements?
2. What is the likelihood that Bernard Landry will hold another referendum on Quebec sovereignty within the foreseeable future? How would the vote go if it were held today?

Chapter 3

CUBA[1]

ISSUE DEFINITION

The United States and Canada have very different policies toward Cuba, with U.S. policy aimed at isolating the Cuban government and Canadian policy espousing constructive engagement. Canada opposed 1996 U.S. legislation that strengthened U.S. sanctions on Cuba because it maintains that certain provisions constitute an extraterritorial application of U.S. law. At the same time, however, both Canada and the United States have taken strong stances in speaking out on Cuba's poor human rights record. Beginning in 1999, Canada became increasingly vocal about human rights in Cuba.

BACKGROUND AND ANALYSIS

The Bush Administration has continued the U.S. policy — in place since the early 1960s — of isolating Communist Cuba, with the objective of bringing about political and economic change. The principal tool of U.S. policy remains comprehensive economic sanctions, which were made stronger with the 1992 approval of the Cuban Democracy Act (P.L. 102-484, Title XVII) and the 1996 approval of the Cuban Liberty and Democratic Solidarity Act (P.L. 104-114), commonly referred to as the Helms/Burton legislation. Another component of U.S. policy consists of measures of support for the Cuban people. These include U.S. private humanitarian

---

[1] Prepared by Mark P. Sullivan, Specialist in Latin American Affairs, CRS Foreign Affairs, Defense, and Trade Division.

donations, U.S. government support for democracy-building efforts for Cuba, and U.S.-sponsored radio and television broadcasting to Cuba.

The Helms/Burton law has two significant provisions that have been opposed by U.S. allies, including Canada. Title III of the law allows U.S. nationals to sue for monetary damages in U.S. federal court those persons who traffic in U.S. property confiscated by the Cuban government. Just as President Clinton did, President Bush has suspended the right to file lawsuits under Title III at six-month intervals as provided under the law. Title IV of the law denies admission to the United States to aliens involved in the confiscation of U.S. property in Cuba or in the trafficking of confiscated U.S. property in Cuba. To date, the State Department has banned from the United States a number of executives from three foreign companies — including Sherritt International, a Canadian mining company — because of their investment in confiscated U.S. property in Cuba.

Canadian policy toward Cuba can be described as supporting political and economic change through engagement and dialogue while at the same time promoting Canadian commercial interests. Canada has maintained diplomatic relations since the 1959 Cuban revolution. Trade relations between the two nations increased in the late 1970s and early 1980s, declined somewhat in the 1980s, but picked up again in the 1990s. In 2000, Cuba exported $275 million in goods to Canada, making it the third leading destination for Cuban exports after the Netherlands and Russia; while it imported $229 million in goods from Canada, making Canada its fifth largest import market *(Direction of Trade Statistics Yearbook,* 2001, International Monetary Fund). Canadian investment in Cuba has increased since the early 1990s, with major investments in the mining and tourist sectors. Canada is also the largest source of tourists for Cuba, with some 350,000 Canadians visiting Cuba in 2001 ("Cuba: Tourism and other Services", *EIU Country Reports,* February 11, 2002).

The Chrétien government initiated a more active policy toward Cuba beginning in 1994. As part of the initiative, Cuba became eligible for official development assistance. Official contacts and exchanges increased as did government financing for Canadian trade and investment. Canada signed a broad agreement with Cuba in 1997 that called for cooperation in a number of areas such as human rights and economic reform. Prime Minister Chrétien paid a state visit to Cuba, the first since former Prime Minister Trudeau visited in 1976.

Canadian relations with Cuba began to cool in 1999, however, and Canada became increasingly vocal about Cuba's poor human rights situation. In March 1999, Cuba's conviction of four leading dissidents led to tension in

Canada's relations with Cuba. Prime Minister Chrétien had asked for the four dissidents' release when he visited Cuba in 1998, but instead the four received sentences ranging from 3½ to 5 years. Chrétien strongly criticized Cuba for the convictions. Lack of Cuban progress on human rights led to Canada's decision not to extend an invitation to Cuba to attend the third Summit of the Americas held in Quebec in April 2001. Then Foreign Minister John Manley maintained that Cuba was "not ready to participate in the summit because it lacks a commitment to democratic principles" ("Manley Courting Bush with his Cold Shoulder to Cuba," *Hamilton Spectator*, March 29, 2001).

STATUS OF THE ISSUE

Canada has strongly objected to provisions in the Cuban Liberty and Democratic Solidarity Act. Specifically, Canadian officials have asserted that Title III of the measure is an extraterritorial application of U.S. law that is contrary to international legal principles, and that Title IV appears to violate chapter 16 of the North American Free Trade Agreement (NAFTA) which covers the temporary entry of business persons. When the United States enacted the Cuban Democracy Act in 1992, a measure which prohibits U.S. foreign subsidiaries from engaging in trade with Cuba, Canada responded by enacting a blocking order under its Foreign Extraterritorial Measures Act (FEMA). After the 1996 enactment of the Helms/Burton legislation, Canada amended FEMA to include a declaration that no judgement under the legislation would be recognized or enforced in Canada. A "clawback" provision was added to allow Canadians to recover in Canadian courts any amounts awarded under the Helms/Burton legislation. While Canada was vocal in its objection to the Helms/Burton legislation, it did not officially challenge the issue in multilateral forums. In 1996, Canada held consultations with the United States under the dispute settlement procedures of the NAFTA, but did not officially challenge provisions of the law under NAFTA. Nor did Canada officially join the European Union (EU) challenge to the Helms/Burton legislation in the World Trade Organization (WTO).

On April 3, 2002, a U.S. Federal Court in Philadelphia convicted Canadian businessman James Sabzali for violating the U.S. trade embargo on Cuba. Sabzali, who is scheduled to be sentenced on June 28, 2002, became a U.S. resident in 1996 and worked for a Pennsylvania-based company, Bro-Tech Corporation, that sold water-purification chemicals to

Cuba. Of the 20 counts against Sabzali for violating U.S. trade sanctions, eight reportedly occurred while he was working in Canada. The Canadian government maintained that it was monitoring the situation, although Foreign Affairs Minister Bill Graham acknowledged that U.S. courts have jurisdiction in the case since Sabzali is a U.S. resident. Several Canadian Members of Parliament argue that the case is an affront to Canadian sovereignty, and have called for Prime Minister Chrétien to intervene with President Bush.

QUESTIONS

1. Given Canada's extensive trade and investment linkages with Cuba, to what extent have Canadian companies taken action to advance workers rights in Cuba? To what extent, if any, has the Canadian government taken any action to advocate the concept of responsible business practices and principles for Canadian firms operating in Cuba? What specific practices has Canada sought to advance?
2. What has been the reaction in Canada to the conviction of a Canadian businessman, also a U.S. resident, for violating U.S. trade sanctions against Cuba? Does the Canadian government intend to raise the issue with the Bush Administration?

Chapter 4

U.S. IMPORTS OF CANADIAN SOFTWOOD LUMBER[1]

ISSUE DEFINITION

The U.S. lumber industry has long argued that imports of subsidized Canadian lumber were injuring U.S. producers. A 1996 agreement to impose a fee on lumber imports above a specified quota expired on March 31, 2001, and the U.S. lumber industry filed countervailing and antidumping petitions to restrict Canadian lumber imports. In March 2002, after negotiations on a solution collapsed, the U.S. Department of Commerce determined that Canadian subsidies amounted to 19.34% of lumber sale value, and that dumping margins averaged 9.67%. In May, the U.S. International Trade Commission determined that Canadian imports had injured the U.S. lumber industry. These determinations lead to a duty of 29% on most Canadian softwood lumber imported into the United States.

BACKGROUND AND ANALYSIS

U.S. lumber producers have periodically expressed concerns about imports of subsidized Canadian lumber. The Department of Commerce (DOC) has investigated the imports several times over the past two decades. In 1981, it found that Canadian subsidies were *de minimis* (insignificant). However, in 1986, its preliminarily finding was subsidies of 15% of sale

---

[1] Prepared by Ross W. Gorte, Natural Resource Economist and Senior Policy Specialist, CRS Resources, Science, and Industry Division.

values; the expected duty was supplanted by a Memorandum of Understanding (MOU), with Canada imposing a 15% export tax on softwood lumber. Canada withdrew from the MOU in 1991, arguing that the provinces had responded to the previous concerns. The next investigation led to a 6.51% duty in 1992, but this duty was successfully challenged under the U.S.-Canada Free Trade Agreement. In 1996, the United States and Canada reached a 5-year softwood lumber agreement — a fee on lumber imports from four Canadian provinces in excess of a specified quota.

Tension between the United States and Canada over softwood lumber trade may be inevitable. Both countries have extensive forest resources, but vastly different population levels and development pressures; vast stretches of Canada are still largely undeveloped, while less area in the United States (outside Alaska) remains relatively pristine. These differences have led to divergent forest policies. In Canada, 90% of the forests are owned by the provincial governments, which have allocated and priced timber to encourage development of the extensive timber reserves. In the United States, 58% of timberlands are privately owned, and private markets dominate the allocation and pricing of timber. U.S. federal and other government-owned forests are regionally important, but the timber is typically sold in a competitive market.

U.S. lumber producers assert they have been injured by Canadian subsidies that have given Canadian lumber producers an unfair advantage in selling lumber in the U.S. market. Canadian provincial stumpage fees (for the right to harvest trees) are asserted to be subsidized — less than their fair market value. The provinces generally use leases and administered fees to allocate and price their timber. Administered fees are unlikely to match market values, but determining whether the fees are significantly below market values, as asserted by U.S. lumber producers, has been controversial, because of differences in tree species, sizes, and grades; in measurement systems; in requirements on harvesters; in environmental protection; and in other factors.

Log export restrictions in British Columbia are also said to be subsidies, because they assure more supply (less competition for timber and thus lower costs) for Canadian producers. Evidence from the U.S. Pacific Northwest, where private logs can be exported but public timber cannot, indicates substantially higher prices for exported logs. However, Canada has challenged as GATT violations the U.S. treatment of log export restrictions as subsidies.

Injuries to U.S. lumber producers are difficult to establish decisively, although the U.S. International Trade Commission (ITC) has found injury every time it has examined the issue. Canada's share of the U.S. lumber market has risen substantially, from less than 7% in the early 1950s to more than 35% in the mid-1990s. Under the 1996 agreement, the quantity of imports has continued to rise, but the market share has been relatively stable. The impact of restrictions on U. S. lumber prices is not easily estimated, but restrictions have probably put upward pressure on U.S. lumber prices. However, the price rise estimated by a group opposed to restrictions would probably have a minor impact on housing costs, and lumber prices are currently lower than the average over the past decade.

STATUS OF THE ISSUE

The 1996 U.S.-Canada softwood lumber agreement expired on March 31, 2001. On April 2, the U.S. Coalition for Fair Lumber Imports filed antidumping and countervailing duty petitions asking the DOC to investigate Canadian lumber imports again. In August, the DOC issued a preliminary determination that subsidies amounted to 19.31 % of sale value, and in October issued a preliminary determination that dumping margins averaged 12.58%. After negotiations for a solution collapsed, DOC issued final determinations on March 22, 2002, that subsidies were 19.34% of sale value and average dumping margins were 9.67%. On May 3, the ITC determined, by a 4-0 vote of the commissioners, that the U.S. lumber industry has been injured by softwood lumber imports from Canada. An import duty averaging 29% will be imposed when the final ITC determination is printed and the DOC has published notice of the duty in the *Federal Register*.

The Bush Administration will face continuing pressure from the U.S. lumber industry and environmental groups to uphold the restrictions on lumber imports, and from homebuilders and other lumber users to terminate the restrictions. In the 107th Congress, concurrent resolutions have been introduced in the House and the Senate both opposing and supporting restrictions on Canadian lumber imports; legislation could still be introduced to require or prevent the Administration from restricting imports. In addition, Canada is expected to challenge the duties under NAFTA (the North America Free Trade Agreement) and before the World Trade Organization (WTO).

QUESTIONS

1. Do Canadian producers have a significant cost advantage because of Canadian timber practices and/or subsidies? Should Canadian practices be modified to enhance competition for timber? Do the systems and situations vary sufficiently to warrant different responses to each Canadian province? What might be the environmental consequences of various possible changes?
2. What options and opportunities do U.S. and Canadian lumber producers, government agencies, and other interested parties have to comment on and to challenge investigations and decisions made under U.S. trade law? Would a NAFTA challenge follow the pattern of the 1982-1984 process, leading to overturning the duties? How might current Canadian challenges before the WTO affect implementation of U.S. trade law, generally as well as specifically for softwood lumber trade? What other WTO challenges might result from continued rancor over lumber imports, and how might these challenges affect other products being traded?
3. How might U.S. trade law be changed to enhance or hinder prospects for restrictions on lumber imports? Should an agreement be negotiated to replace the U.S. duties? Should, and could, such an agreement encompass all Canadian provinces or just the four major lumber-producing provinces, or should separate agreements be sought between the U.S. government and each province?

Chapter 5

U.S.-CANADA STEEL TRADE[1]

ISSUE DEFINITION

How has the decision of President Bush on March 5, 2002, to impose safeguard tariffs on steel products under Section 201 of the U.S. Trade Act of 1974 affected U.S.-Canadian relations? The U.S. policy has led to a reaction around the world, with numerous U.S. trading partners seeking consultations preparatory to filing cases against the U.S. action with the World Trade Organization (WTO). But the presidential decision specifically exempted imports from the North American Free Trade Agreement (NAFTA) partners, Canada and Mexico, even though both are major steel suppliers to the U.S. market. Consequently, Canada has supported the U.S. Section 201 action, though it is also considering its own safeguard tariffs to protect itself against any diversion of steel imports that would have gone to the United States before the President's Section 201 actions.

BACKGROUND AND ANALYSIS

Canada (4.2 million metric tons, MT) and Mexico (2.7 million MT), our NAFTA partners, ranked second and fourth among steel exporters to the United States in 2001. And Canada is the top source of imported steel, about 15% of the total, if one divides the European Union (EU) into its constituent member states, instead of counting all EU imports together. The North American industry is highly integrated, with many companies operating

---

[1] Prepared by Stephen Cooney, Industry Analyst, Resources, Science, and Industry Division.

across borders. Four of the largest North American steel producers, among those producing more than two million tons of steel per year, are headquartered in Canada (Stelco, Dofasco, Ipsco, and Algoma). The United Steelworkers Union (USWA) operates in both the U.S. and Canada, and Leo Gerard, its president, is from Ontario.

The steel industry in Canada, as well as in the United States, has been going through a recent period of economic difficulties, especially among the integrated steelmakers, who produce steel directly from iron ore. One of the major Canadian producers, Algoma, has only just emerged from bankruptcy. Both the USWA and the broadest U.S. industry association, the American Iron and Steel Institute, called for Canada to be exempted from Section 201 trade relief. Both Canada and Mexico had been exempted by the Clinton Administration from the limited Section 201 trade actions on steel line pipe and wire rod products in 2000. Other WTO partners protested how this was done, and U.S. domestic competitors subsequently gained a ruling from the U.S. International Trade Commission (ITC) that NAFTA imports contributed to injury suffered by American companies. But in November 2001, President Bush reaffirmed the continued exclusion of the NAFTA trading partners from trade relief in that case.

President Bush was pressed by many Members of Congress, union representatives and steel companies to address the question of the broader impact of imports on the steel industry. On June 5, 2001, he announced that his Administration would call upon the ITC to begin an investigation under Section 201 of U.S. trade law, which authorizes the imposition of temporary safeguard tariffs in accordance with WTO rules. He also announced that he would seek multilateral negotiations with U.S. trading partners on fundamental issues of global steel overcapacity and government subsidies to the steel industry. The ITC investigation divided the Bush request into 33 product segments, grouped into four broad categories, accounting for about three-quarters of all U.S. steel imports: carbon and alloy flat, long, and pipe and tube products, and stainless and tool steel products. The ITC conducted a six-months-long investigation. It was required to find that imports were a substantial cause or threat of injury ("not less important than any other cause"), before it could recommend remedy relief. Without a finding of injury, the President cannot implement tariffs under Section 201. This provision of law may be applied to all imports, and, unlike the antidumping and countervailing duty law widely used by the U.S. steel industry, requires no finding of unfair trading practices.

The ITC found that imports were a substantial cause of injury in about half of the 33 product groups. Under NAFTA it must also make separate determinations on products of Canadian and Mexican origin. For five products, the ITC found that Canadian imports contributed to injury done to U.S. producers. These included two carbon and alloy long products (hot-rolled and cold-finished bar), carbon and alloy tubular fittings and flanges, and stainless steel rods and fittings. On one more product with respect to Canadian imports (welded pipe), the ITC tied, leaving President Bush an option whether to include it in remedies. The ITC reported its findings and remedy recommendations to the President in December 2001.

On March 5, 2002, at the end of the Section 201 process, the President announced a series of temporary trade relief measures to safeguard the U.S. steel industry against injury from imports. President Bush exempted all Canadian and Mexican products from the Section 201 remedy measures. The maximum duties established by the President were 30% in year one of a three-year period. But imports from Canada and Mexico are exempt from all safeguard duties.

Canadian International Trade Minister Pierre Pettigrew "welcomed" the decision to exclude Canada from Section 201 tariffs, noting that the six categories cited by the ITC covered about $Cdn. 1.9 billion in Canadian steel exports, out of a total of $3.6 billion. Moreover, the consequences of the Bush decision mean that, "Not only is it expected that U.S. domestic steel prices will rise, but Canada, as an unrestricted supplier into the U.S., will be in a unique position to take advantage of those higher prices," according to the official press release of Canada's Department of Foreign Affairs and International Trade. However, citing a threat of diversion of steel from the U.S. market, Canada, also announced the consideration of its own safeguard measures on steel imports. The Canadian industry and union urged safeguards against any diversion of steel from the U.S. market. On March 22, 2002, the Canadian government initiated its own safeguard investigation in response.

Two other steel issues over the past year have affected U.S.-Canadian relations. Under the "Byrd Amendment" in P.L. 106-387 of 2000, U.S. petitioners in antidumping cases may claim their share of antidumping duties from cases in which they participated. About half of the $207 million in disbursements in 2001 went to steel companies. Canada has joined ten other U.S. trading partners in filing a WTO case against this law. A decision is due in July 2002. Also, the Bush Administration in 2001 initiated a case on iron ore and semi-finished steel slabs under Section 232 of U.S. trade law, a rarely used provision that allows the President to impose relief against imports whose impact is found to be a threat to U.S. national security. Canada is one of the leading suppliers of U.S. iron ore imports. However, the

Department of Commerce reported in October 2001 that such imports were not a national security threat and no action was taken under this statute.

STATUS OF THE ISSUE

Canada is continuing its own review on the imposition of safeguard measures against imports from countries diverting product from the U.S. market. Meanwhile, Canada has been very active in urging the U.S., the EU and other participants to continue discussions at the Organization for Economic Cooperation and Development regarding the reduction of global steel capacity and the agreement of discipline on rules for steel trade and subsidies - such an approach was tried, but failed in the early 1990s. The OECD talks were threatened by the U.S. Section 201 decision and the strongly adverse EU reaction.

QUESTIONS

1. Opponents of U.S. safeguard steel tariffs have said that such protection will ultimately cost more jobs in steel-consuming industries than will be saved in the steel industry, and at a high cost in the national economy. What is the view in Canada on safeguards costs and benefits?
2. The United States and Europe have each offered capacity cuts of about 20 million tons in the context of the OECD discussions on steel. What is Canada prepared to offer with respect to the issue of retiring uncompetitive plants and reducing global overcapacity?

Chapter 6

CULTURAL ISSUES[1]

ISSUE DEFINITION

Canada's geographic proximity to the United States and its relatively small population and economy have led to fears among some Canadians that their culture and identity are in danger of being overwhelmed by the United States. The Canadian government has responded to this fear by imposing certain restrictions on cultural content (print, film, video, music, radio, and television media). In addition, as a bilingual nation, Canadian and several provincial governments subsidize the development and propagation of French language content. Canada supports the cultural exemptions in the North American Free Trade Agreement (NAFTA) and the World Trade Organization (WTO). U.S. officials and the U.S. entertainment industry consider such restrictions as protectionist, and they have sought to open up the Canadian market to further U.S. penetration.

BACKGROUND AND ANALYSIS

In the past, both countries have tried to avoid disputes over cultural issues. Bilateral trade in this sector is very small compared to total U.S.-Canadian trade of goods and services, which totaled $380 billion in 2001. Moreover, such contentious disputes can damage the bilateral relationship in other areas. The cultural sector is exempted from both the U.S.-Canada Free Trade Agreement (CUSTA) and the North American Free Trade Agreement

---

[1] Prepared by Ian F. Fergusson, Analyst in International Trade and Finance, Foreign Affairs, Defense, and Trade Division.

(NAFTA), which superseded the CUSTA. However, each country is allowed to take "measures of equivalent commercial effect" for trade actions in the cultural sector inconsistent with the NAFTA. In other words, the United States could retaliate with restrictions against other Canadian products when Canada invokes the cultural exemption to restrict trade.

The Government of Canada maintains that its restrictions on trade or investment are necessary to maintain the commercial viability of firms or industries that are crucial to preserve Canada's cultural identity. It claims that the small Canadian home market does not provide the economies of scale necessary to compete with larger U.S. entertainment or media conglomerates. Without such indigenous cultural promoters, or the restrictions that make them possible, native talent would remain undiscovered at home or ignored in the U.S. market. According to U.S. policymakers, such restrictions are protectionist and have little to do with maintaining Canada's cultural identity, but instead deny opportunities to similar U.S. firms, which are very successful in global markets. The United States is also concerned that Canadian trade restrictions for cultural purposes, if unchallenged, may set precedents for other countries to impose or continue similar restrictions.

MEDIA RESTRICTIONS

Numerous restrictions apply to Canadian media carriers to promote Canadian content. For example, Canadian content requirements are specified in radio, television and cable broadcasting as well as in direct-to-home satellite broadcasting. For example, a private Canadian television broadcaster must devote 60% of its overall schedule, and 50% of its prime time schedule to Canadian content, as determined by the Canadian Radio-Television and Telecommunications Commission (CRTC). Policies requiring that distribution rights to feature films be acquired from Canadian distributors also seek to encourage domestic production. Any proposed foreign direct or indirect acquisition of a cultural firm must be reviewed by the federal government to ensure "net benefit to Canada." Restrictions on investment by U.S. firms in Canadian-owned film distribution companies include a prohibition on foreign takeovers and limitations on investment in new distribution firms.

PRODUCTION OF U.S. FILMS IN CANADA

Recently, the U.S. film industry has taken advantage of Canadian tax incentives and the high exchange rate between the U.S. dollar and the Canadian dollar and has shifted more filming of U.S. movies and television programs to Canada, a phenomenon known as "runaway production." Several Federal and provincial tax incentives and subsidies are specifically designed to promote Canadian cultural content, yet others are intended to promote the film industry as a source of employment and revenue. Some in the United States have proposed that the federal government, as well as the states, enact similar tax credits to stem runaway production. A study commissioned by the Directors Guild of America and the Screen Actors Guild estimated that runaway production cost the U.S. economy $10.3 billion and a loss of 20,000 full-time jobs in 1998, five times more than it was in 1990. Based on data supplied by the Directors Guild of Canada, Canadian officials have argued that Canada accounts for only 2% of the production, but 10% of the consumption, of the films and TV programs produced in the two countries. Canadians contend that their tax incentives do not violate any agreement with the United States, that they are similar to those offered by many U.S. states, and that Canadian venues are popular to U.S. producers because they offer good economic and production value.

INTERNET POLICY

The Canadian government is responding to the internet revolution with policies designed to promote Canadian content and French language presence on the internet, and to promote the development of Canadian e-commerce. In 1999, the CRTC decided not to extend regulatory oversight to the internet, implicitly acknowledging the difficulty in regulating the origin of internet content. Instead, the government has concentrated on efforts to promote a domestic digital and creative content industry, which can then disseminate Canadian content in new media venues.

STATUS OF THE ISSUES

The United States Trade Representative continues to monitor Canada's cultural content restrictions for protectionist regulations. On runaway production, numerous U.S. states have enacted tax incentives or other programs to encourage film production, and legislation to provide incentives has been introduced in the California legislature. In addition, legislation was introduced in both chambers of Congress in 2001 (S.1278, H.R. 3131) to provide a 25% wage credit for the first $25,000 of income to each employee of qualified independent film and television productions. In addition, the Screen Actors Guild and several union locals involved in film productions filed a countervailing duty petition against Canada in late 2001, but the filing was withdrawn in January 2002. One potential problem with using trade remedies against Canadian film practices is that countervailing duty procedures in U.S. trade law apply only to trade in goods, yet film production traditionally has been considered a service.

QUESTIONS

1. Is there evidence that Canadian trade and investment restrictions in cultural industries help to preserve Canada's cultural identity?
2. When Canada invokes NAFTA's cultural exemption, is it taking a risk of retaliation against other products by the United States? Is there concern in Canada that the costs of invoking the cultural exemption (U.S. retaliation against other products) may exceed the benefits?
3. Some Canadian tax incentives for production of film and TV programs do not appear to be aimed at protecting Canadian culture, but at stimulating the Canadian economy. Do such incentives encourage or discourage filming by Canadian companies, or are they neutral?
4. To what extent does the relatively low value of the Canadian dollar (C$1.00=$.64 on May 7, 2002) contribute to runaway production?

Chapter 7

NORTH AMERICAN INTEGRATION[1]

ISSUE DEFINITION

The terrorist attack of September 11, and its aftermath, have sparked a wide-ranging debate in Canada over its relationship with the United States, including the feasibility or desirability of furthering the process of North American integration. The extent to which the two economies are integrated was dramatized by the havoc wreaked on trade flows by border closings occurring after the terrorist attacks. While concerns in the United States over the U.S.-Canada border are focused primarily on border security and immigration issues, the debate in Canada has become much broader, encompassing such issues as the nature of sovereignty, the desirability and feasibility of further economic integration with the United States, and even the adoption of the U.S. dollar. This discourse is not unusual in Canada; questions concerning its relationship with the United States continually loom large in policy discussions. However, additional factors such as the recent trade disputes with the United States, combined with several perceived slights, have caused some political leaders and commentators to attach a new urgency to this discussion.

BACKGROUND

The most immediate economic effect of the terrorist attacks on the border was the extensive delays on commerce caused by increased security

---

[1] Prepared by Ian F. Fergusson, Analyst in International Trade and Finance, Foreign Affairs, Defense, and Trade Division.

precautions. Trade between the United States and Canada is conducted primarily by track, and 4 border crossings in Ontario and one in British Columbia make up 75% of the volume of trade. Backups at the Ambassador Bridge (Detroit-Windsor) reportedly stretched thirty-six miles into Ontario. Both Canada and the United States implemented measures to return commerce to normal. On December 12, 2001, the United States and Canada announced a joint "Smart Border Declaration" consisting of measures to improve the flow of peoples and goods, to improve the physical infrastructure of the border, to coordinate information and enforcement resources. (Please see Border Security Issues, by Lisa Seghetti.)

However, some aspects of increased cooperation with the United States on border and immigration issues have proved controversial to some Canadians. These questions generally have taken the form of resistance in some quarters to the notion of harmonization of United States and Canadian regulations. A segment of Canadian public opinion fears that harmonization of customs and immigration regulations would inevitably lead, due to the wide disparity in population and economic power of the two nations, to adoption of U.S. standards, and implicitly, the policies behind them. Moreover, Canadian resistance to this harmonization, according to this view, could imperil the economic relationship with the United States. However, others contend that Canadian and U.S. regulations affecting the border are more similar than different and would be for the most part compatible. Hence, the scope of coordination in certain areas of border management may be acceptably encompassed by mutual recognition.

Others in Canada believe the lesson from September 11 is that increased cooperation with the United States is both necessary and inevitable, given the reality of Canadian trade flows and economic interdependence. Yet, they believe such integration must be managed to assure Canada maintains its interest and its sovereignty. Several long-term economic options have received renewed attention, including a *customs union, a common market,* or a *monetary union.* The latter also has received attention due to the long-term slide of the Canadian dollar, despite the recent uptick in strength of the currency. These concepts are not new, and they have been discussed in conjunction with "deepening" the North American Free Trade Agreement (NAFTA). Consequently, these discussions often involve Mexico as well.

The first step usually discussed regarding the further integration of the North American economy is the creation of a *customs union.* Members of a customs union commonly eliminate tariffs among themselves, and erect common barriers against the rest of the world. Both the U.S. and Canada have already eliminated all tariffs between each other under NAFTA, and have similar, though not identical, tariff schedules with third countries. Because all customs duties would be paid at port of entry at the perimeter of the customs union, the need for customs agents whose purpose is to collect revenue would be obviated. However, border agents also enforce immigration, sanitary and phytosanitary, and environmental laws. A customs union does not imply a harmonization or mutual recognition of each nation's regulations. Thus, a national presence at the border would continue to be necessary. It is also unclear in what form current trade remedy practices could be continued under a customs union. Such actions against third countries could continue relatively easily if both sides found it necessary; however, actions against each other would require the continued payment of duties at the border.

COMMON MARKET OR ECONOMIC UNION

Deeper integration of the North American economic space would imply some form of common market or economic union. A common market area would add free movement of labor and capital; thus, immigration and investment regulations would need to be harmonized or mutually recognized. In addition to a common tariff policy and free trade in goods and services, a common market would imply free movement of capital and labor. At this point, harmonization of certain investment and immigration issues would need to be agreed upon. A type of economic union approaching that of the European Union would also require harmonized or mutually recognized standards and regulations and perhaps some supranational institutions. Although the United States and Canada share many developed country level standards, this form of integration would still need to be meticulously worked out. For example, would the United States adopt the metric system to fulfill its obligations to harmonize standards? Could the two nations adopt common forestry prices and management policies that are at the heart of the softwood lumber dispute? Would either nation allow supranational entities to overrule laws passed by Congress or Parliament? These questions illustrate the extent to which North American economic integration would affect the governance of the United States, Canada, and possibly Mexico.

MONETARY UNION

Another discussion recurrent in many Canadian policy circles is that of monetary union with the United States. This potential goal has been discussed in many forms. The Canadian dollar could be linked in value to the U.S. dollar; Canada could adopt the U. S. dollar; or a new North American currency (called the Amero by one proponent) could replace the U.S. and Canadian dollars, and perhaps the Mexican peso. The Canadian dollar (or loonie, named for the bird on the C$1 coin) steadily has depreciated in value in the last twenty years. Worth approximately $.84 at the time of the U.S. Canada Free Trade Agreement in 1989, recently the loonie has been trading at around $.64. The underlying weakness of the loonie has been blamed on several factors. Some economists attribute its weakness to soft commodity and natural resource markets, which make up a disproportionate share of its trade. Others maintain that the loonie is destined to remain a second-tier currency, perpetually in the shadow of the U.S. dollar. In addition, the Canadian government's austere fiscal and monetary policies (made unavoidable by the legacy of massive spending and borrowing in the 1970s and 1980s), has paradoxically weakened demand for the currency, because the government, which continues to run surpluses, has stopped issuing new sovereign debt.

As with most economic phenomena, a depreciated currency has its advantages and disadvantages. A weak loonie makes Canada's exports of goods and services relatively cheaper and makes it an attractive destination for tourists. However, imports and traveling abroad become relatively expensive for Canadians. It also makes Canadian assets relatively cheap and more attractive to foreign investors. This can lead to increased foreign investment, but it can also lead to foreign takeovers of domestic firms. This latter point has raised concerns that Canada is losing its indigenous corporate base through foreign takeovers and acquisitions. Evidence of this phenomenon has been demonstrated by the disappearance of a number of firms on the Toronto Stock Exchange and the loss of company headquarters to the United States. In addition, this spring Deputy Prime Minister John Manley cited the low dollar as a reason for lackluster productivity gains in Canadian industry, yet he also questioned the ability of Canadian firms to compete if the loonie increased in value.

Those who support monetary union with the United States argue that it would force Canada to make the necessary structural adjustments that would make Canada competitive with the United States. In other words, dollarization or a currency union would remove the ability to cushion adverse economic conditions through depreciation of the currency. By tying the loonie to the U.S. dollar or in adoption of the dollar outright, Canada would be making the unmistakable commitment to converge with U.S. macroeconomic policy. Then Canada would be able to reap the benefits of U.S. policy, which traditionally have been lower inflation, lower interest rates, and higher levels of growth than Canada has experienced. In addition, the savings in trade transaction costs would be significant for the volume of trade the two nations conduct.

Opponents of monetary union contend that monetary union would lead to an unacceptable loss of political and economic sovereignty. Monetary policy would be dependent on (or tied to) actions of the U.S. Federal Reserve. Thus, the Canadian government would be left with fewer levers to combat inflation or fight recession. In a monetary union in which macroeconomic convergence is reached, this point may not be important. To opponents of monetary union, however, the two economies respond differently to events, and thus need to utilize different adjustment mechanisms. Furthermore, with a population and economy smaller than some Federal Reserve districts, the ability of Canada to influence U.S. monetary policy in a monetary union would be small.

STATUS OF THE ISSUE

The active pursuit of North American integration is not a front-burner issue for either the United States or Canadian government. However, these Canadian proposals, although longstanding, have been intensified by the disruption of the two economies after September 11 by the closure of the border. They reflect a realization that the security requirements of the border have an economic component, and that perhaps Canada can use its security cooperation in the war against terrorism to gain economic security that greater integration would bring.

QUESTIONS

1. Has Canadian enthusiasm for monetary union or dollarization been tempered by the meltdown of the Argentine economy, another country who adopted and then abandoned its tie to the dollar?

2. Is it possible to achieve a "deepening" of NAFTA at Mexico's current stage of development? Is it politically possible at this point to exclude Mexico from any economic integration proposals?
3. How do the recent trade disputes over steel and softwood lumber and the passage of the recent U.S. farm bill affect your perception of further economic integration between the two (three) countries?

Chapter 8

CANADA AND THE FREE TRADE AREA OF THE AMERICAS (FTAA)[1]

ISSUE DEFINITION

Canada has played an active role in the formulation and negotiation of the Free Trade Area of the Americas (FTAA). Last year, Canada hosted the third Summit of the Americas in Quebec City on April 20-22, 2001. Leaders of 34 hemispheric nations approved a plan to complete negotiations on the FTAA agreement by January 2005 and to implement an agreement by the end of 2005. A preliminary bracketed text was discussed at the Summit, and a bracketed, working text was released in July 2001. At the summit, the governments pledged to continue to work to alleviate poverty, to foster education, to strengthen environmental standards, to promote compliance with core labor standards and to combat drug trafficking. The nations also agreed to a democracy clause that stipulated that an "interruption of the democratic process" in a country was 'an insurmountable obstacle' to that nation's participation in the FTAA process.

The Free Trade Area of the Americas process began at the first Summit of the Americas, held in Miami in 1994. At this Summit, hemispheric leaders agreed to create an FTAA by 2005. The second Summit, held in Santiago, Chile in 1998, launched the FTAA negotiations in accordance with the San Jose Ministerial declaration of March 1998. If completed, the FTAA would encompass an area with a population of 800 million people and a combined

---

[1] Prepared by Ian F. Fergusson, Analyst in International Trade and Finance, Foreign Affairs, Defense, and Trade Division.

gross domestic product of in excess of $11 trillion: the largest preferential free trade area in the world.

Canada has been an active participant in the FTAA process. In addition to hosting last year's summit, Canada served as the first Chair of the negotiating process from May 1998 to October 1999, culminating in the November 1999 Toronto Ministerial. Canada has played a leadership role in negotiations concerning government procurement, competition policy and e-commerce. It has also been instrumental in promoting the participation of civil society in the negotiating process, and it led attempts to make public the bracketed text of the Agreement.

In addition to participation in formal FTAA negotiations designed to construct a comprehensive trade agreement, Canada has negotiated bilateral free trade agreements with Chile (implemented in July 1997) and Costa Rica (signed April 23, 2001). Negotiations are also underway with sub-regional groupings such as Mercosur (the Southern Cone Common Market), the Central American Common Market (El Salvador, Guatemala, Honduras, Nicaragua), and Caricom (the Caribbean free trade area). While the FTA with Chile, and to a more limited extent Costa Rica, are roughly patterned after the North American Free Trade Agreement (NAFTA), they also contain significant differences and omissions which could influence the characteristics of any eventual FTAA.

BACKGROUND AND ANALYSIS

It is only within the last ten years that Canada has taken a significant interest in Latin American affairs. This condition has been variously ascribed to Canada's historic orientation, toward Europe, its ties to Great Britain and the Commonwealth, its preoccupation with the U.S. relationship, and its lack of cultural affinity with Latin America, save for the French and English speaking Caribbean. In fact, Canada did not join the Organization of American States until 1993. Neither is Canada's interest in the Americas south of the United States based on current trade patterns. Two way trade with the Americas, outside the United States and Mexico, totaled approximately $5 billion in 2001, or only 3% of Canada' s trade. Canada has a stock of foreign direct investment of about $45 billion in the region, but investments in Bermuda, Bahamas and Barbados exceed that of Brazil, Chile and Venezuela, the three leading recipients of Canadian foreign direct investment in South America.

An FTAA agreement would benefit certain important export sectors in the Canadian economy. While 94% of goods trade freely between Canada and potential FTAA countries, there are significant bound tariffs on paper products, potash, information technology, automotive parts, and non-tariff barriers on many service sectors. Canadian officials stress the potential for future increases in trade and investment between Canada and Latin America under FTAA. Some Canadians also see the FTAA as a way to become less dependent on trade with the United States, which accounted for 85% of two way trade in 2001.

Canada's involvement in the FTAA and Latin America can also be seen in the context of traditional aspirations of Canadian foreign policy. Canada has often played the role of mediator, both between Britain and other Commonwealth countries, and between the United States and the rest of the world. It has often undertaken foreign policy initiatives based on moral imperative, rather than self-interest. In this case, Canada is promoting free trade as a just cause, a policy that promotes democracy, development, as well as the expansion of commerce.

The FTAA has been advocated in Canada as a way to rectify some perceived weaknesses in NAFTA and to reinvigorate the Agreement. Some contend that the ten year old agreement must be updated to account for changed circumstances in such areas as border issues, energy transmission, and regulatory issues related to the increased integration of the three economies. Others would like to see the FTAA process challenge U.S. agricultural policies, and antidumping and countervailing duty policies.

One potential area of revision that has become a sensitive issue for Canada is NAFTA's investor rights provisions (Chapter 11). This provision allows companies to sue government entities for making policy decisions that put firms at a competitive disadvantage. Chapter 11 has been utilized by companies in a series of well publicized cases, including one in which Federal Express brought suit against Canada Post over the latter's courier service. Opponents of FTAA have expressed the concern that this provision could threaten the future provision of services provided by the Canadian government, including the Canada Health Service.

Canada's opportunities to influence the FTAA process may be hampered by several factors. First, Canada and the United States agree on far more than they disagree. Both countries share developed country outlooks which are expressed in similar positions on labor, environment, and the role of civil society. Both countries oppose the use of sanctions to enforce labor and environmental provisions of trade agreements. Second, attempts to formulate negotiating alternatives to U.S. positions depend on good relations with Brazil, a leading skeptic of the FTAA process. Yet, Canadian relations with Brazil have been strained by a series of recent trade disputes. Third, Canada may have less resources in terms of negotiating teams and support to devote to FTAA if a new round of WTO negotiations is undertaken. Fourth, the perception that Canada doesn't have much at stake may diminish Canada's influence among countries whose societies may be transformed by such an agreement.

STATUS OF THE ISSUE

Organizers of the Quebec Summit hope that the Action Plan adopted at its conclusion will provide momentum for the negotiations set to begin in May 2002. However, there are still substantial disagreements among the parties, and negotiations among 34 nations to remove myriad trade barriers will be extremely complex. Progress towards an FTAA may also be influenced by the delegation of Trade Promotion Authority by the Congress to the President.

QUESTIONS

1. Some observers and administration officials maintain that FTAA negotiations will not make substantial progress without the adoption of Trade Promotion Authority? Do you agree?
2. Is there enthusiasm among the Canadian public for the FTAA? Do Canadian negotiating positions on the FTAA reflect a vision for the development of hemispheric relations? What are some of the Canadian public's concerns about the FTAA process or this vision?
3. What is the Canadian government's position on provisions concerning investor rights in the FTAA? Are there other provisions of NAFTA that the government would like to redress in the FTAA process?
4. How does Canada believe labor and environmental issues should be addressed through the FTAA process?

Chapter 9

CANADA AND THE WORLD TRADE ORGANIZATION[1]

ISSUE

A signatory to the Havana Treaty in 1947, Canada was one of the founding members of the General Agreement on Tariffs and Trade (GATT). Over the intervening half-century, Canada has become a leading trading economy and has become increasingly involved in shaping the world trading system through several rounds of GATT and now World Trade Organization (WTO) negotiations. Most recently, Canada played a key role in facilitating the launch of the Doha Development Round. The Doha Ministerial Declaration set forth objectives in several issue areas to be negotiated with a completion date of January 2005. In the run-up to the Doha agreement, Canada also contributed to formulating certain developed country negotiating positions as a member of the Quad group (United States, the European Union, Japan, Canada).

BACKGROUND AND ANALYSIS

Canada's interest in the world trading system partly can be attributed its dependence on it. In the half-century since the signing of the GATT, Canada has developed an export driven economy. In 1947, Canada exported approximately 2% of its GDP; by 2000, that figure reached 46% of GDP. It

---

[1] Prepared by Ian F. Fergusson, Analyst in International Trade and Finance, Foreign Affairs, Defense, and Trade Division.

was recently estimated that one-third of Canadian employment is directly dependent on international trade. The United States is Canada largest trading partner, taking 86% of its exports and sending 76% of Canada's imports. It must be noted, however, that much of this trade relationship is due more to the Canada-U.S. Free Trade Agreement of 1988 (which was incorporated into the North American Free Trade Agreement in 1994), than to multilateral trade liberalization.

Negotiations on the Doha Development Round are in their early stages in Geneva. While detailed positions in these negotiations are still being formulated, each party, including Canada, has submitted negotiating objectives for the round. In Canada, the House of Commons Standing Committee on Foreign Affairs and International Trade (SCFAIT) recently issued a report containing several recommendations for the government to consider in developing Canada's negotiating positions. These statements and recommendations illustrate Canada's priorities in the upcoming negotiations.

Agriculture

Canada and the United States broadly share common objectives concerning agricultural negotiations begun in early 2000. Canada seeks to eliminate all export subsidies, to seek maximum reductions or elimination of trade distorting domestic support, to improve market access for agricultural products, and to negotiate new disciplines on export taxes. The SCFAIT also recommends the adoption of a "development box" that would allow developing countries to exempt certain food security crops from market access considerations, to provide more support to farmers, and to protect their farm sectors from import surges.

Industrial Market Access

Canada's main objectives in tariff negotiations are to seek broad-based market access opportunities, especially among developing countries where tariffs on non-agricultural products remain high. It seeks to negotiate sectoral agreements on chemicals, forestry products, non-ferrous metals, fisheries and an expansion of products under the Information Technology Agreement (ITA).

Services

Negotiations on amending the General Agreement on Trade in Services (GATS) have been in progress since early 2000. Canada's stated objective is to target sector requests to maximize the opportunities of Canadian service exporters, especially small and medium enterprises (SMEs). Conversely, Canada is committed not to negotiate on liberalizing the provision of services relating to its health care, education, or social services. Canada has also declared that its cultural identity policies (including Canadian content restrictions and media subsidies) will not be subject to the GATS, but instead it has proposed the negotiation of a "New International Instrument on Cultural Diversity" that would place disciplines on and govern regulations concerning cultural industries.

Trade Remedies

The launch of negotiations at Doha to discipline, to clarify, and to provide transparency in the use anti-dumping, subsidies, and countervailing measures is a key priority for Canada. The government's position in these negotiations is to separate legitimate uses of trade remedy legislation from disguised attempts at protectionism. The SCFAIT report noted the trend in developing countries to use anti-dumping measures without transparency or due process was "disturbing" and that curbing such practices was "an urgent priority of the world trading system." In addition, Canada has objected to the use of these remedies by the United States and has been engaged in disputes over softwood lumber, tomatoes, and steel safeguards. However, both the United States and Canada agree on the necessity of addressing fishing subsidies in these negotiations, especially with regard to use by developing countries.

Dispute Settlement

The Canadian government supports the dispute settlement process and notes that it has generally worked well. However, it favors negotiations to shorten dispute time frames, to increase compliance incentives, and to reduce the incidence of retaliatory action in unresolved disputes. The SCFAIT report considers the open defiance of panel reports by losing parties as threatening the confidence in the whole dispute settlement process.

STATUS OF THE ISSUE

Agreement on the negotiating structure for the Doha Development Round was reached in February 2002, including the appointment of chairs to the negotiating committee. The Canadian representative to the WTO, Sergio Marchi, was named Chairman of the body's General Council, which oversees the negotiations. The fifth ministerial meeting will be held in late 2003. It will assess the progress of the negotiations and is scheduled to be concluded in January 2005.

QUESTIONS

1. The theme of the Doha Development round is the integration of developing and least-developed countries into the world trading system. While this is a laudable goal, many key exports of developing countries, such as textiles and apparels, face high tariffs and quotas. How does Canadian trade policy seek to resolve this conundrum?
2. Given that 85% of Canadian exports go to the United States, and are thus covered by NAFTA, how important are the WTO negotiations to the Canadian government, and to the Canadian people? Do the WTO talks present Canada with the opportunity to remedy perceived weaknesses in NAFTA? If so, in what areas?
3. 3.What is the legislative process in Canada for approving trade agreements? Are there legislative procedures analogous to Trade Promotion Authority, or fast-track procedures, currently being debated in the U.S. Senate?
4. Will the U.S. farm bill, which increases subsidies to U.S. farmers, adversely affect Canadian farmers? Has passage of this measure, which some claim runs counter to the WTO, along with other recent trade disputes with the United States such as softwood lumber and the steel safeguard action, made Canadians wary of negotiating further trade measures with the United States?

Chapter 10

WHEAT TRADE[1]

ISSUE DEFINITION

U.S.-Canadian agricultural trade is important to both countries and has been growing in both directions. Despite a U.S.-Canada Free Trade Agreement (FTA) which dates from 1989 and an agreement on agricultural marketing opening measures reached in December 1998, there are several points of friction in the bilateral agricultural trading relationship. Large imports of spring and durum wheat have been viewed as especially problematic by producers in U.S. border states, especially when U.S. wheat prices are low.

The combination of low U.S. wheat prices and large imports of Canadian durum and spring wheat has been a source of concern to U.S. wheat producers who think that imports have had a large negative impact on grain prices. U.S. grain producers have expressed concern about the potential of the Canadian Wheat Board (CWB), a state-trading enterprise (STE), to practice price discrimination and to operate in a nontransparent way. Despite studies that have concluded that the CWB has the potential to cross-subsidize grain sales in different markets, little evidence has been adduced to indicate that the CWB is engaging in unfair trading practices.

Market access of U.S. wheat into Canada also has been of concern. However, the U.S. Department of Agriculture (USDA) and the Canadian Ministry of Agriculture have reported progress in dealing with market access issues under the December 1998 agricultural market opening agreement (the Record of Understanding or ROU). Progress, according to the two

---

[1] Prepared by Charles E. Hanrahan, Senior Specialist in Agricultural Policy, CRS Resources, Science and Industry Division.

ministries, includes facilitation of transhipment of U.S. wheat through Canada to final destinations in the United States. As of October 1999, certificates of origin had been issued for the movement of 550,000 tons of wheat and other grains through Canada.

BACKGROUND AND ANALYSIS

Canada is the second largest market for U.S. agricultural exports (after Japan) and the leading source of U.S. agricultural imports. Since the U.S.-Canada Free Trade Agreement (FTA) came into force in 1989, total (two-way) U.S. Canadian agricultural trade has increased from a combined total of $5 billion in 1989 to $17.5 billion in 2001. U.S. agricultural exports to Canada increased from $2.2 billion in 1989 to $8 billion in 2001. U.S. imports of Canadian agricultural products increased from $2.8 billion in 1989 to $9.5 billion in 2001. Trade liberalization following the 1989 FTA (subsequently incorporated into NAFTA) contributed to the expanded agricultural trade. However, not all of the change in U.S.-Canadian agricultural trade can be attributed to the FTA or to any other single factor. Weather, policy changes, and world supply and demand conditions are some of the factors that have affected U.S.-Canadian agricultural trade. Exchange rates are also an important factor. Prevailing exchange rates between the Canadian and U.S. dollars make Canadian imports cheaper for U.S. buyers and U.S. farm products more expensive for Canadian buyers.

Not addressed by the ROU were the operations of the CWB. On September 8, 2000 the North Dakota Wheat Commission (NDWC) asked the Office of the U.S. Trade Representative (USTR) to investigate the CWB for allegedly discriminatory price activities in both U.S. and third-country markets. USTR agreed to launch an investigation under Section 301 of the Trade Act of 1974. The NDWC requested relief for U.S. wheat producers from Canadian wheat imports through a quota, tariff-rate quota (TRQ) or voluntary restraint. Meanwhile, Canadian agriculture, trade, and CWB officials denied that the CWB engages in price discrimination and called for dismissal of the 301 investigation.

In response to the NDWC petition, the U.S. Trade Representative conducted a 16 month investigation. During the course of the investigation, USTR requested that the U.S. International Trade Commission (USITC) conduct an exhaustive investigation of the wheat trading practices of the CWB. (USITC published its study, *Wheat Trading Practices: Competitive Conditions between U.S. and Canadian Wheat,* USITC Publication 3465,

September 2001.) Based in part on the information developed in the USITC report, USTR concluded that the Government of Canada grants the CWB special monopoly rights and privileges which disadvantage U.S. wheat farmers and undermine the integrity of the trading system. USTR's further concluded that the CWB's monopoly has taken sales from U.S. fanners, and is able to do so because it is insulated from commercial risks, benefits from subsidies, has a protected domestic market and special privileges, and has competitive advantages due to its monopoly control over a guaranteed supply of wheat.

USTR announced (February 15, 2002) that it would pursue a four-pronged approach to deal with the CWB. USTR will:

- Examine taking a possible dispute settlement case against the CWB into the World Trade Organization (WTO);
- Work with the NDWC and the U.S. wheat industry to examine the possibilities of filing U.S. countervailing duty and antidumping petitions;
- Work with industry to identify specific impediments to U.S. access to Canada's wheat market; and
- Pursue reform of monopoly state trading enterprises (STEs) in WTO agriculture negotiations.

The NDWC, U.S. Wheat Associates, and the National Association of Wheat Growers all welcomed USTR's findings, although reportedly they were disappointed that USTR did not recommend imposing a TRQ on Canadian wheat imports.

The Canadian Government and the CWB both expressed disappointment with USTR's findings. Canada's minister responsible for the CWB said that "the report released by the USITC shows clearly that the continuing allegations against the CWB really are without basis. The ITC, after an extensive fact-finding investigation, found that the CWB is neither undercutting prices, nor over-delivering value in the United States. Since 1990, the CWB has been subjected to eight other investigations, and its trading practices have always been cleared." Some Canadian officials suggested that if the USTR had hard evidence of violation of trade rules, USTR would have recommended the imposition of a TRQ on Canadian wheat imports as requested by the NDWC.

STATUS OF THE ISSUES

USTR has rejected imposing a TRQ on Canadian wheat imports as a violation of U.S.-Canadian trade agreements. USTR also has not established a time table for deciding about the initiation of a dispute settlement case in the WTO or for initiating antidumping or countervailing duty actions. There is some disagreement as to whether the ITC investigation would support an antidumping action. CWB officials say that ITC's finding that Canadian wheat prices were higher than U.S. prices over the period of investigation would make it difficult to establish dumping. U.S. observers, however, point to factors such as the large volume of wheat imports into the United States as supporting an antidumping charge. According to some, the Uruguay Round Agreement on Agriculture's "Peace Clause," which calls for WTO members to exercise "due restraint" in taking trade remedy actions, could prevent the United States from proceeding with countervailing duties. Based on considerations such as these, the most likely course of action for USTR, according to trade analysts, is for the United States to pursue establishing disciplines on STEs in WTO agriculture negotiations. The European Union and a number of agricultural exporting countries have allied themselves with the United States in seeking greater discipline over STEs.

QUESTIONS

1. How will Canada respond to challenges to the CWB as a result of USTR's section 301 investigation?
2. What is Canada's position on applying greater disciplines and more transparency in the operations of STEs, like the CWB?
3. Are there ways in which the CWB could become more transparent in its operations so as to reduce informational uncertainties about its operations?

Chapter 11

DAIRY TRADE[1]

ISSUE DEFINITION

In Canada, dairy producers receive an allotment for sales of milk on the domestic market at a high, administered price. Production in excess of this allotment or quota can be sold at a lower price as commercial export milk – CEM – to companies who process milk for export. The United States and New Zealand have argued in WTO dispute settlement that the system constitutes an export subsidy and that it enables Canada to exceed its export subsidy reduction commitments for processed dairy products, especially cheese. The issue is important for several reasons. First the issue has commercial importance for U.S. and New Zealand dairy exporters who maintain that the CEM system is an export subsidy that gives Canada an unfair competitive edge in world dairy markets. U.S. and New Zealand trade officials estimate that the CEM scheme costs them each around $35 million a year in lost exports. The most recent WTO ruling on this matter also raises the issue of the definition of an export subsidy and the latitude it might give countries to support export sales at below domestic prices. Finally, the case reveals a potential defect in the WTO dispute settlement process in not allowing an appellate panel to remand a decision to the original dispute panel. This issue has been in WTO dispute settlement since 1997.

---

[1] Prepared by Charles E. Hanrahan, Senior Specialist in Agricultural Policy.

BACKGROUND AND ANALYSIS

The United States and New Zealand first challenged Canada's dairy program in the WTO in 1997. Canada had established a Special Milk Classes Scheme (SMCS) in 1995. Under the scheme, the government fixed prices for milk used in processed dairy products for export at a much lower level than milk destined for the Canadian market. As a result, exporters were able to sell their dairy products abroad at world market prices. Earnings from the exports were pooled with returns from domestic sales and shared among Canadian milk producers. The effect of the SMCS, according to the United States, was to enable Canada to exceed its export subsidy reduction commitments for dairy products agreed to in the URAA.

The United States requested consultation with Canada on the SMCS in October of 1997. When consultations did not yield a resolution of the dispute, the United States and New Zealand in February 1998 requested the formation of a WTO dispute panel to rule on its complaint that the SMCS constituted an export subsidy which enabled Canada to exceed its export subsidy reduction commitments under the URAA. The United States also charged that Canada's administration of its tariff-rate quota (TRQ) on fluid milk violated the 1994 WTO Agriculture Agreement as well as the WTO's Agreement on import licensing. Under the TRQ, Canada limited fluid milk imports to 64,500 tons annually and limited imports under the quota to products packaged for consumer use that were valued at less than C$20 per consumer. (A TRQ permits entry of specified quantities of product from a given country over some specified period at zero or a low tariff rate, while imports above the quota amount face higher, usually prohibitive, tariffs.) The panel was established March 25, 1998.

The WTO dispute panel ruled (in March 1999) that by making discounts on milk for processors contingent on use in exports, the assistance provided under the SMCS constituted an export subsidy under the URAA. In particular, the assistance constituted a direct subsidy in the form of a payment in kind under article 9.1 (a) of the URAA as a result of the discounted milk for export provided by the Canadian government and its agencies. Article 9.1 (a) lists as subject to reduction commitments under the URAA, "the provision of governments or their agencies of direct subsidies, including payments-in-kind, to a firm, to an industry, to producers of an agricultural product, to a cooperative or other association of such producers, or to a marketing board, contingent on export performance." The panel ruled that the SMCS also constituted a direct subsidy in the form of payments on the export of agricultural products by virtue of government action as set out in Article 9.1(c). According to Article 9.1(c), export subsidies are subject to reduction commitments if they are "payments on the export of an agricultural product that are financed by virtue of governmental action whether or not a charge on the public account is involved, including payments... on an agricultural product from which the exported product is derived."

Therefore, the panel reasoned, dairy product exports financed through the SMCS are subject to the reduction commitments made by Canada under the URAA. Since the quantity of exports exceeded the export reduction commitments made by Canada in the URAA, the panel concluded that Canada had violated its obligations under the Agreement. In addition, the panel found that the assistance provided under the SMCS constituted a circumvention of Canada's subsidy reduction commitments under Article 10.1 of the URAA.

With regard to the second U.S. complaint about the administration of Canada's TRQ for fluid milk, the panel also ruled that Canada's measures violated WTO provisions.

Canada appealed the panel's decisions, and the appellate panel in the case on October 13, 1999 essentially upheld the earlier dispute settlement panel's decisions regarding the SMCS and exports. Although it overturned some aspects of the earlier ruling, the appellate panel upheld the original panel's main conclusion that Canada's practice of setting lower purchasing prices for milk used in processed dairy products for export constitutes an export subsidy subject to reduction commitments under Article 9.1(c) of the WTO Agreement on Agriculture. In this connection, the appellate panel agreed with the original panel that the provincial marketing boards are government agencies regardless of the make up of the boards. While the provincial boards do retain a "high degree of discretion in the exercise of their powers," the governments retain "ultimate control" over them, and their regulatory function is enforceable by the law of the state, making them governmental in nature, according to the appellate panel. In addition, the appeals panel said, government action is "indispensable" to ensure the supply of milk to processors for export.

The appellate panel overturned the panel's finding that Canadian authorities had no right to restrict imports of fluid milk in its TRQ to consumer-packaged milk for personal consumption by Canadians. In other words, the panel found that Canada could restrict purchases of fluid milk to those made by individual consumers who had crossed the border. But, the appellate panel also concluded that Canada could not limit such purchases to C$20.

Canada agreed to bring its dairy program into compliance with the WTO ruling and announced its compliance plan on January 3, 2001. Canada replaced its federal system with nine systems in milk-producing and exporting provinces. According to the announced plan, decisions to sell milk for the export market will be made by individual producers based on commercial grounds only, with quantities, prices, and other terms and conditions negotiated between producers and processors/exporters. Under the plan, processors will submit bids and farmers submit offers to a bulletin board administered by a third party contractor to the provincial milk marketing board. In Ontario, there will be only one third-party administrator, while in most other provinces there may be multiple third-party contractors.

The United States and New Zealand questioned the legality of the new scheme and argued that the Canadian federal milk export subsidy program was being replaced by governmentally-mandated programs in nine Canadian provinces that will allow Canada to maintain exports of dairy products at the same levels as under the WTO-inconsistent federal scheme. U. S. dairy groups complained that the new provincial programs still would make milk available to processors for export at prices below those charged for milk for domestic consumption and require that all discounted milk made available to processors be exported. U.S. dairy industry representatives pointed out that it is unlawful in Canada to sell milk for domestic consumption at prices lower than those established by the marketing boards. This, according to various U.S. dairy sources, means that the revised dairy export regime still constitutes an export subsidy under WTO rules (Article 9. l(c))

In February 2001, the United States, New Zealand, and Canada agreed on procedures for handling the milk export dispute. Consultations were held as required in WTO dispute settlement. Following consultations, the United States and New Zealand requested authorization for retaliation against Canada, which by mutual agreement was tabled (i.e., postponed), pending a WTO compliance review which was completed in July of 2001.

The WTO compliance review panel ruled that the provincial arrangements set up in Canada for the export of milk used in processed dairy products continue to provide export subsidies. The panel found that Canada exceeded its export subsidy cap for cheese during the 2000-2001 marketing year. Cheese exports were 10,666 metric tons as of April 2001, well above the quantity limit of 9,076 fixed for the 2000-2001 marketing year. Canada appealed the panel's ruling.

The appeals panel, in its ruling issued on December 3, 2001, found that the earlier panel ruling (of July 2001) against Canadian milk management policies was flawed because the panel did not use the right benchmark for determining whether subsidy payments were made. Because the compliance panels review was flawed, the appellate panel said it was unable to rule on the consistency or inconsistency of Canada's dairy programs with its obligations under WTO agreements. As a result of this ruling, the Canadian milk scheme stands, because the appeals panel could not determine whether it was consistent with WTO rules.

According to the decision of the appellate panel, the benchmark that should be used to determine whether exports are subsidized is the cost of production, not the domestic price for milk or the world price. The appellate report also raised a question about whether domestic support measures could spill over and erode countries' export subsidy commitments. The appeals panel noted: "We believe that it would erode the distinction between the domestic support and export subsidies disciplines of the Agreement on Agriculture if WTO-consistent domestic support measures were automatically characterized as export subsidies because they produced spill-over economic benefits for export production." The comparison between administered domestic prices and export prices as a benchmark for determining whether exports are subsidized tended to collapse the distinction between the two categories of WTO disciplines, according to the appeals panel. While the United States may want clarification of what exactly constitutes an export subsidy in WTO agreements, some suggest that too broad a ruling on the impact of domestic support measures on export subsidy commitments could impugn U.S. support programs that use administered prices to provide domestic support. *(Inside U.S. Trade,* January 4, 2002.)

The issue of remanding appellate decision to original panels is one that may be taken up in negotiations on reforming dispute settlement in the Doha Development Agenda (DDA) round.

STATUS OF THE ISSUE

Following the appellate panels's report, the parties to the dispute (the United States, New Zealand, and Canada) reached an agreement to allow a second WTO compliance panel to revisit the dispute. Although Canada argued that establishing a new compliance panel, an unprecedented move in WTO dispute settlement, potentially created "an endless loop of litigation," it did not block the move. That new compliance review panel was established on December 18, 2001 and began its review on February 18, 2002. A ruling should be made 90 days thereafter (around mid-May 2002). If the panel rules against Canada, WTO arbitration on the U.S.-New Zealand request for $70 million in annual sanctions would begin immediately and a decision on the level of retaliation would be issued within the following 60 days. If the panel finds that Canada is in compliance, yet another appeal by the U.S. and New Zealand could be initiated.

QUESTIONS

1. What approach to revising its dairy export scheme could Canada take if the compliance review determines that it is inconsistent with Canada's WTO obligations?
2. What is Canada's position in WTO negotiations about further trade liberalization for dairy products?

Chapter 12

BORDER SECURITY ISSUES[1]

ISSUE DEFINITION

Prior to the events of September 11, the focus on border security was beginning to shift from immigration-related issues, to issues related to facilitating legitimate cross-border commerce. The events of September 11, however, have directed Congress' attention to U.S.-Canada border security-related issues. Both countries are now striving to balance adequate border security with other issues such as the facilitation of legitimate cross-border travel and commerce, and protecting civil liberties. Congress may address several border security-related issues pertaining to the U.S.-Canada border. These may include (1) more information sharing with Canada, including joint intelligence sharing; (2) greater sharing of technology such as fingerprint data and passport readers; (3) off-site pre-inspection and pre-clearance areas for certain categories of frequent travelers (i.e., business and employment-related travelers); and (4) the expansion of the dedicated commuter lane program for low-risk frequent travelers.

BACKGROUND AND ANALYSIS

Many observers maintain that historically, the U.S.-Canada border has been understaffed and lacks the necessary infrastructure to adequately screen individuals seeking entry into the United States. An Office of Inspector General (OIG) report issued in February 2000 highlighted deficiencies with

---

[1] Prepared by Lisa M. Seghetti, Analyst in Social Legislation, Domestic Social Policy Division.

the INS border patrol along the northern border. Among other things, the OIG report asserts that "the border patrol faced significant enforcement challenges along the United States-Canada border and was unable to adequately respond to illegal activity, primarily because of a lack of sufficient staff and resources." According to an October 1, 2001 Senate hearing on *Northern Border Security,* INS has 334 border patrol agents and 498 inspectors assigned to the northern border compared to over 9,500 border patrol agents and inspectors assigned to the smaller southern border.

Congress took action to address the aforementioned problems by passing the USA PATRIOT Act (P.L. 107-56) on October 26, 2001. The Act authorizes the Attorney General to triple the number of INS border patrol personnel and inspectors along the northern border and authorizes $50 million for INS to make technological improvements and to acquire additional equipment for the northern border. Pending legislation, as well as the recently passed Border Security and Visa Entry Reform Act of 2002 (H.R. 3525), would similarly authorize additional personnel and technological and infrastructure improvements at the borders.

The U.S. and Canadian governments signed a declaration establishing a "smart-border" on December 12, 2002. The declaration includes a 30-point plan to secure the border and facilitate the flow of low-risk travelers and goods through coordinated law enforcement operations, intelligence sharing, infrastructure improvements, the improvement of compatible immigration databases, visa policy coordination, common biometric identifiers in certain documentation, prescreening of air passengers, joint passenger analysis units, and improved processing of refugee and asylum claims, among other things. Previously, on December 3, 2001 the two countries signed a joint statement of cooperation on border security and migration that focuses on detection and prosecution of security threats, the disruption of illegal migration, and the efficient management of legitimate travel.

Other efforts to increase border security between the U.S. and Canadian government include the 1999 *Canada-U.S. Partnership Forum* (CUSP) and the February 24, 1995 joint accord, *Our Shared Border.* CUSP provides a mechanism for the two governments, border communities and stakeholders to discuss issues of border management. The guiding principles for U.S.-Canada cooperation resulting from these dialogues are as follow:

- Streamline, harmonize and collaborate on border policies and management;

- Expand cooperation to increase efficiencies in customs, immigration, law enforcement, and environmental protections at and beyond the border; and
- Collaborate on common threats from outside the United States and Canada.

The 1995 accord brought together four agencies (the Immigration and Naturalization Service, United States Customs Service, Revenue Canada, Citizenship and Immigration Canada, and the Royal Canadian Mounted Police) to focus on joint border issues such as enhancing security through more effective inspection efforts that target specific problem areas (e.g., drugs, and smugglers), and the continued commitment to pool inspection and enforcement resources.

Section 110 Automated Entry/Exit Control System

Section 110 of the Illegal Immigration and Immigrant Responsibility Act (IIRIRA; Division C of P.L. 104-208) required the Attorney General to develop an automated system to record the entry and exit of every alien arriving in and departing from the United States. This provision became a source of concern for border communities whose members feared that if Section 110 were implemented it would cause gridlock at border crossings. Consequently, Congress amended Section 110 in the Fiscal Year 1999 Omnibus Consolidated Appropriations Act (P.L. 105-277) by extending the deadline for the implementation of an entry/exit system and by prohibiting significant disruption of trade, tourism, or other legitimate cross-border traffic once the entry/exit system is in place. And in June 2000, Congress further amended Section 110 in the Immigration and Naturalization Service Data Management and Improvement Act of 2000 (P.L. 106-215) by delaying the immediate implementation of the entry/exit system at all ports of entry and requiring the development of a system that uses available data to record alien arrivals and departures, without establishing additional documentary requirements. The events of September 11, however, have redirected Congress' attention to the immediate development and implementation of an automated entry and exit control system at all ports of entry. In his fiscal year 2003 budget, President Bush has requested $362 million for such a system.

Machine-Readable, Tamper-Resistant Entry and Exit Documents

Congress recently passed the Enhanced Border Security and Visa Entry Reform Act of 2002. Section 303 of the act would require the Attorney General and the Secretary of State to issue machine-readable, tamper-resistant visas and travel documents that have biometric identifiers by October 26, 2004. It also would require the installation of biometric identifier readers and scanners at all ports of entry by October 26, 2004.

QUESTIONS

1. Congress recently passed legislation that would require the development and implementation of biometric identifiers for travel documents. The Canadian government has fast tracked the implementation of a machine-readable, permanent fraud-resistant resident card for new immigrants. Will the new technology be compatible with the U.S. documents, that is will the Canadian cards have similar biometric identifiers that are unique to the card holder? If not, should they have similar biometric identifiers?
2. Congress has passed legislation that would require an automated entry and exit system at all ports of entry that records arrivals and departures of every alien entering and exiting the country (Section 110 of the Illegal Immigration and Immigrant Responsibility Act, IIRIRA; Division C of P.L. 104-208). Has the Canadian government considered similar tracking of aliens entering and leaving the country?

Chapter 13

IMMIGRATION AND REFUGEE POLICIES[1]

ISSUE DEFINITION

Should the United States be concerned that Canada's immigration and refugee laws and policies pose a threat to national security? If so, what types of changes would be most welcomed in the United States, and what types of bilateral agreements would best protect North America from terrorist infiltration through lawful entry? Of particular importance in this regard is the question of what effects an agreement to require potential refugees to present their claims in the first safe country of entry might have.

BACKGROUND AND ANALYSIS

Although Canada does not have country or worldwide quotas, immigration levels are set out in annual targets. In 2000, the global target was in the range of 210,000 to 235,000 and approximately 250,000 immigrants were granted permanent residence. The target for 2002 is slightly higher and the Government has announced that it would eventually like to increase this total to approximately 300,000 a year. That figure would be almost 1% of the total Canadian population and is subject to Canada's absorptive capacity. Asian countries, such as China, India, Pakistan, and the Philippines, are heavily represented at the top of the list of countries that Canada's immigrants come from, but no one nation dominates. Immigrating to Canada is often difficult and is usually time-consuming. Screening is

---

[1] Prepared by Stephen F. Clarke, Senior Legal Specialist in the Western Law Division, Law Library of Congress.

reported to be quite thorough. Canada employs a points system to assess applicants. Changes were recently announced that were aimed at attracting more highly skilled and educated immigrants. Canada already accepts a much higher percentage of independent immigrants and a much lower percentage of family class immigrants than the United States does.

One notable feature of Canadian immigration is that over half of the persons accepted settle in the three largest cities of Toronto, Montreal, and Vancouver. This tendency, combined with the high rate of immigration, has raised some concerns, particularly among security agencies, about destructive "diaspora nationalism" emerging in the concentrated communities. However, this situation is not unique to Canada and opposition to immigration has not been voiced nearly as loudly or as forcefully in that country as it recently has in parts of Western Europe. In fact, the high profile of diverse immigrant communities has generally come to be seen as a distinguishing feature that Canadian society that promises growth in what would otherwise be a declining population.

Canadian policy for asylum applicants is a far more contentious issue in Canada than immigration, not so much for its negative effects within Canada, but because it is generally seen to invite fraud and abuse. During the past several years Canada has received approximately 25-30,000 asylum applicants per year. In 2001, this number increased to approximately 45,000 refugee claimants with about 44% of the applications considered being accepted. This is higher than the corresponding figure in the United States. Of particular concern to Canadian officials is the fact that approximately 40% of the overall total and some 70% of port of entry claimants enter Canada through the United States. There is significant evidence that illegal migrants are abusing the U.S. Non-Immigrant Visa system to access North America and the Canadian asylum system to stay here. One reason for this is that Canada detains few undocumented refugee claimants pending independent identification and the federal and provincial governments grant immediate assistance to claimants who have not yet substantiated their claims. The result is that the majority of Canada's refugee claimants arrive in Canada without any documents and are allowed free entry into the country even though it is clear that many purposely disposed of the documents they had or received while entering the United States. Canada has significantly increased the use of detention and up-front security screening of such claimants before the decision is made to release or detain these people. New facilities are being prepared, but opposition critics have contended that even stronger action needs to be taken.

The Canadian refugee system was recently portrayed as being extremely liberal in a 60 Minutes piece that attracted considerable attention in Canada. Mention was made of four well-known cases of terrorists from the Middle East who entered Canada as refugees with the intention of launching attacks against United States targets. Among these was the case of Ahmed Ressam who was arrested two years ago while crossing the border with explosives that he planned to set off at Los Angeles airport. Also highlighted were the cases of suspected terrorists who have remained in the country for years while fighting their way through a very lengthy appeal process. ("North of the border, Canada becoming a staging ground and a fund-raising base for hundreds of terrorists around the world." April 28, 2002). It is important to realize, as in the United States, people deemed to be either a flight risk or a danger to security can be detained. Moreover, the Supreme Court of Canada recently ruled that persons linked to terrorist organizations can be deported to countries where they might face torture when security concerns so require.

The 60 Minutes segment elicited a wide range of responses. While a number of commentators agreed that the United States has good reason to fear that Canada's refugee policies can be easily employed by terrorists to enter North America, others contended that terrorists are more likely to use other means to enter both Canada and the United States. Many writers pointed out that there is no evidence that any of the September 11th hijackers had a Canadian connection and that the refugee system has essentially been used for "queue jumping" by enterprising persons who might not qualify under the country's immigration laws. Persons of this view questioned how great the security risk to the United States could be if a significant number of claimants are coming from this country. Within the House of Commons, the opposition Canadian Alliance called on the Government to begin turning back undocumented refugee claimants entering from the United States, but the Government rejected the suggestion that it should take such a unilateral action.

Canada has enacted a new Immigration and Refugee Act. This law is scheduled to go into effect in June. One of the major objectives of the drafters of the legislation was to create a mechanism for weeding out frivolous refugee claims. At the same time, provision was made for expanding the appeals process in other cases. For people deemed a danger to security, the access to appeals is significantly reduced.

STATUS OF THE ISSUE

Canada and the United States are currently working on two agreements that officials hope to complete by the end of June. One agreement would more closely coordinate visa policies. The other would allow both countries to turn back undocumented refugee claimants at the border unless they have a compelling reason to present their claims in one country instead of the other. The desire to reunite with family members might be such a reason.

A safe third country agreement could substantially reduce the number of refugee claims presented by undocumented persons in Canada, but it would not address problems presented by "boat people" and others who attempt to conceal their identities while traveling to Canada through other countries. A safe third country agreement could also result in an increase in refugee claims being presented in the United States.

In recent years, Canada's courts have extended many rights and protections to refugee claimants, frustrating some attempts by the Government and quasi-judicial officers to eliminate some abuses. Thus, in formulating new refugee policies, Canadian officials, like their counterparts in the United States, have to carefully consider other legal requirements.

QUESTIONS

1. Can Canada enter into a meaningful safe third country agreement that will withstand judicial scrutiny on both legal and constitutional grounds? Can a holding up of the implementation of such an agreement through lengthy appeals over how broadly the exceptions should be interpreted be avoided?
2. Canadian officials often point out that most refugee claimants enter Canada from the United States. However, aside from expanding visa requirements and restrictions, what steps can the United States take to frustrate claimants who are bent on availing themselves of the more generous Canadian system?
3. Are the well-reported cases of terrorists and potential terrorists who have entered North America through legal means a sign of a potentially much greater threat? How much support, including financial support, do terrorist groups have in the new immigrant communities?
4. What effect do Canadian officials believe the adoption of the new immigration law will have on detention policies?

Chapter 14

U.S.-CANADA PACIFIC SALMON MANAGEMENT[1]

ISSUE DEFINITION

U.S. and Canadian attention currently focuses on how the provisions of a 1999 agreement relating to the Pacific Salmon Treaty are being implemented, with rising concerns for possible threats from fish farming of Atlantic salmon. Pacific salmon management under the U.S.-Canada Pacific Salmon Treaty's principles is complicated because salmon migrate widely along the coast, often living and feeding for years in waters under a different jurisdiction from where they were spawned, and because fisheries often intercept salmon spawned in another state or nation. After years of controversy, an agreement under the 1985 bilateral Pacific Salmon Treaty between the United States and Canada was concluded in June 1999. This understanding resolved differences so as to permit negotiation of harvest agreements under the various species-specific provisions of Treaty Annex IV.

BACKGROUND AND ANALYSIS

As expressed in Article III, the two basic principles of the Pacific Salmon Treaty are the conduct of fisheries and salmon enhancement programs to: 1) prevent overfishing and provide for optimum production,

---

[1] Prepared by Eugene H. Buck, Senior Analyst in Natural Resources Policy, CRS Resources, Science, and Industry Division.

and 2) provide for each Party to receive benefits equivalent to the production of salmon originating in its waters. In addition, Parties are to take into account: 1) the desirability of reducing interceptions, 2) the desirability of avoiding undue disruption of existing fisheries, and 3) annual variations in stock abundance.

In the mid-1990s, Canada claimed the United States was not abiding by the Treaty's "benefits equivalent" or equity obligations. Since the total U.S. catch of Canadian-origin salmon generally exceeds the total Canadian catch of U.S.-origin salmon, Canada believed that the United States should reduce its harvest. The United States' objectives became fractured when Alaskan state interests differed from those of the Pacific Northwest states (Washington-Oregon) and tribes. Alaska's harvest of some salmon species had been high due to record and near-record levels of salmon abundance, at a time when harvest in some Pacific Northwest salmon fisheries was at near-record lows, due to poor survival of coho and chinook salmon. Complicating the issue is the fact that a significant proportion of the chinook salmon caught in Southeast Alaska waters are fish returning to rivers in Canada and the Pacific Northwest.

This conflict was complicated because many of the fishing companies operating in Alaska and British Columbia are either owned by the same parent company or are subsidiaries. A large quantity of Alaskan-caught salmon is processed in Prince Rupert, British Columbia, while significant amounts of Canadian-caught sockeye salmon are processed in Blaine and Bellingham, Washington. Also, many offshore corporations buying salmon for Japan have operations in both countries. In addition, many U.S. permit holders for southeast Alaska commercial fisheries are non-residents of Alaska, and a large number of U.S. citizens participate in Canadian recreational fisheries.

Four main areas of controversy characterized the recent conflict: 1) how to divide Canada's Eraser River sockeye salmon harvest between British Columbia and Washington State fishermen, including tribal/aboriginal interests; 2) how to manage the Canadian sport and commercial fishery off Vancouver Island that both a) intercepts coho and chinook salmon bound for Washington and Oregon and b) can adversely affect the conservation of Canadian stocks; 3) how to manage the Southeast Alaska commercial and sport fishery that intercepts intermingled chinook salmon bound for British Columbia and Southeast Alaska drainages, as well as rivers in Washington and Oregon; and 4) how to account for Canadian sockeye salmon that are harvested incidentally in Alaska's Noyes Island seine fishery for pink salmon of Alaskan origin, primarily during *El Nino* events.

After many years of heated diplomatic struggles, on June 3, 1999, U.S. and Canadian officials announced a new comprehensive agreement to resolve longstanding disputes and to ensure implementation of the conservation and harvest-sharing principles of the Pacific Salmon Treaty. The new agreement established abundance-based fishing regimes for the Pacific salmon fisheries under the jurisdiction of the Treaty; created two bilaterally-managed regional funds to promote cooperation, improve fisheries management, and aid stock and habitat enhancement efforts; and included provisions to enhance bilateral cooperation, improve the scientific basis for salmon management, and apply institutional changes to the Pacific Salmon Commission. Potential problems with U.S. capitalization of the regional enhancement funds were addressed in the FY2000 budget, and language authorizing this funding through FY2003 was enacted in section 628 of P.L. 106-553. Mutual efforts continue positive as the 2002 salmon season approaches, and managers implement the provisions of the 1999 agreement under different conditions.

STATUS OF THE ISSUE

Recently concerns that may complicate management under the Pacific Salmon Treaty have arisen over the perceived threats to wild Pacific salmon from extensive fish farms of Atlantic salmon in British Columbia and Washington State waters. Particularly controversial are proposals to lift a British Columbia moratorium on new fish farming permits and allow expansion of fish farming operations in British Columbia waters. Questions have been raised over the effects of fish farms on the health of wild Pacific salmon and their habitat, arising from 1) escapes of cultivated salmon from net pens, 2) invasion of wild fish habitat by the escaped fish, 3) predation upon juvenile wild salmon by escaped fish, and 4) disease and parasite transmission to wild Pacific salmon.

QUESTIONS

1. What differences will characterize how U.S. versus Canadian fishery managers approach regulation of the 2002 salmon harvest?
2. What actions are necessary during 2002 by both U.S. and Canadian parties to promote sound management of Pacific salmon under the 1999 agreement? What management actions are likely?

3. What bilateral efforts are being undertaken to address concerns about the expansion of fish farming of Atlantic salmon along the Pacific coast?

Chapter 15

WASTE ISSUES

ISSUE DEFINITION

Since 1991, the Canadian province of Ontario has shipped substantial amounts of solid waste to the United States for disposal. Some of the communities on the receiving end of such waste have pressured the Congress for legislation to allow them to restrict out-of-state and out-of-country waste from disposal, thus far without success. Should such waste flows be limited or subject to regulation?

BACKGROUND AND ANALYSIS

Canada and the United States have open borders for waste shipments, and in general, waste has flowed across the border in both directions without incident. The United States does not report data regarding such shipments on a regular basis, but information is available from Environment Canada and from some U.S. states. Available data distinguish hazardous waste from other solid waste. The United States appears to be a net exporter to Canada of hazardous waste, but is a net importer of non-hazardous solid waste.

Hazardous Waste

According to a comprehensive recent report by the Texas Center for Policy Studies (using data from Environment Canada), Canada imported 540,000 tons of hazardous waste (mostly from the United States) in 1998.

Exports of hazardous waste from Canada (mostly to the United States) were about half that amount, 276,000 tons. According to the same report, between 1987 and 1998, Canada's imports of hazardous waste exceeded its exports in 9 of 12 years, including each of the last five years for which data were available. Data from the State of Michigan also show exports to Canada exceeding imports. In 2000 (latest available data), Michigan exported 60,112 tons of hazardous waste to Canada, while imports from Canada to the state totaled 17,106 tons.

Since 1985, the Solid Waste Disposal Act (at 42 U.S.C. 6938) has required exporters of hazardous waste to notify the Environmental Protection Agency and the receiving country. Exporters are required to provide information concerning the types and quantities of waste to be exported, and to report annually the total amount of waste exported to any country. Since 1986, Canada and the United States have also had a bilateral agreement governing hazardous waste exports. This agreement requires both countries to notify each other and provide information concerning the types and quantities of waste to be exported. Environment Canada and the U.S. Environmental Protection Agency are the agencies charged with implementing the agreement.

Non-Hazardous Solid Waste

There are no federal notification or reporting requirements for shipments of non-hazardous waste, including municipal solid waste (MSW), construction and demolition (C&D) waste, medical waste, and non-hazardous industrial waste, nor is there any administrative authority to restrict imports. It is these shipments that have proven controversial, with the controversy apparently now growing.

Although there are no notification or reporting requirements for these wastes at the federal level, many state governments do require the operators of solid waste management facilities to report the origin of waste received for disposal. According to these data, the Canadian province of Ontario appears to have shipped major quantities of such waste (principally MSW and C&D waste) to the United States (particularly Michigan) in recent years.

With the exception of about 50,000 tons of waste destined for an incinerator in Niagara Falls (NY), Ontario did not ship any non-hazardous solid waste to the United States until the summer of 1991. At that time, the U.S. Department of Agriculture rescinded regulations that had prevented land disposal of foreign waste. The change in regulations opened U.S.

disposal sites to Ontario at a time when the cost of disposal had risen to about $110 (U.S.) per ton in the Toronto area. Commercial haulers quickly found lower cost disposal alternatives in the United States, and Ontario exported approximately 1,430,000 tons of waste (including both municipal solid waste and construction and demolition waste) to the United States in 1992. Six states, including Ohio, Pennsylvania, New York, and Michigan, were the principal destinations. Most of the waste was collected by commercial haulers, who exported because disposal in the United States was substantially cheaper than in Ontario. As business disappeared at Metro Toronto landfills, the metropolitan government reversed course. In the summer of 1993, tip fees in the Toronto area were lowered to about $64 (U.S.) per ton. This made disposal in Ontario more attractive, lowering exports to the United States.

In the past year, however, the issue has arisen again. On December 4, 2001, the Toronto City Council voted 38-2 to approve a new solid waste disposal contract that, according to press reports, would ship an additional 1.25 million tons a year of waste to the Carleton Farms landfill in Wayne County, Michigan, beginning in January 2003. The contract would run for three years. In addition, two other Ontario communities that generate a combined 385,000 tons of waste annually have signed contracts to ship their waste to Carleton Farms, according to a source with the Ontario Ministry of Environment and Energy. Waste imports from Ontario had already risen 152% in the past two years, according to the Michigan Department of Environmental Quality, to 1.8 million tons. As a result, waste imports from Canada have become a controversial issue, particularly in Michigan.

STATUS OF THE ISSUE

In the present Congress, several bills have been introduced concerning interstate and international shipments of waste, and hearings have been held by both the Senate Environment and Public Works Committee and the House Energy and Commerce Committee. Three bills have been prominent in discussions of the issue: Rep. Rogers' H.R. 1927, which would allow states to limit or ban receipt of foreign municipal solid waste; H.R. 1213 /S.1194 (Greenwood / Specter), which would prohibit disposal of out of state municipal solid waste and C&D waste unless the receiving facility had a host community agreement, a permit, or a contract specifically authorizing waste imports; and S. 2034 (Voinovich), which is similar to S. 1194 in many respects. No action has been taken on these bills.

QUESTIONS

1. Given the concerns in receiving states over past (and potential) shipments of waste from Canada to the United States, would Canada be willing to work with the United States to develop a bilateral reporting system to measure exports and imports of all kinds of waste between the two countries?
2. Many landfill operators have reached what are called "host community agreements" with local governments, under which the local government receives financial benefits or agreed services in return for accepting out-of-area waste. Should waste imports be limited to communities in which the landfill owner or operator has negotiated a host community agreement with the local government? If so, should the agreement meet some minimum standards (e.g., specifically authorizing waste imports, setting minimum requirements for host community fees, etc.)?

Chapter 16

NORTHERN ENERGY DEVELOPMENT[1]

ISSUE DEFINITION

Should the United States proceed to develop energy resources thought to be in the coastal plain of the Arctic National Wildlife Refuge (ANWR)? And if it chooses to do so, how would Canadian interests, especially those of the Gwich'in people who live on both sides of the Alaska/Yukon boundary, be affected? In a related matter, if the abundant natural gas already known to occur in and around Prudhoe Bay Alaska were to be developed, what path would a pipeline take to bring it out - through Canada, or a wholly Alaskan route? Canada opposes ANWR development, in order to protect the calving grounds of a caribou herd heavily used by Gwich'in in both countries. At the same time, it supports a natural gas pipeline that would travel from Alaska through Canada.

BACKGROUND AND ANALYSIS

One important element of the energy debate in the 107th Congress is whether to approve energy development in the Arctic National Wildlife Refuge (ANWR) in northeastern Alaska, and if so, under what restrictions, or whether to continue to prohibit development in order to protect the area's biological resources. ANWR is an area rich in fauna, flora, and commercial oil potential. Development proponents argue that ANWR oil would reduce U.S. energy markets' exposure to recurring crises in the Middle East; boost

---

[1] Prepared by M. Lynne Corn, Specialist in Natural Resources Policy, CRS Resources, Science, and Industry Division.

North Slope oil production and extend the economic life of the TransAlaska Pipeline System; and create many jobs in Alaska and elsewhere. They maintain that ANWR oil could be developed with minimal environmental harm, with a footprint limited to 2000 acres of a 19 million acre Refuge. Opponents argue that intrusion on this ecosystem cannot be justified on any terms; that it should be designated as wilderness; that oil found (if any) would provide little energy security and could be replaced by cost-effective alternatives; and that job claims are overstated. The House-passed version of H.R. 4 contains a title which would open the area to energy development; the Senate-passed version does not. The bill will be in conference soon.

Canada opposes energy development in the U.S. Arctic National Wildlife Refuge (ANWR) primarily because it might disturb calving of the Porcupine Caribou Herd (PCH). The PCH is covered under the Agreement between the United States of America and Canada on the Conservation of the Porcupine Caribou Herd, which entered into force on July 17, 1987. The objective of the agreement is to conserve the herd for customary, traditional uses by peoples on both sides of the international boundary, with disputes to be settled by consultation between the parties. Since it was an executive agreement, no implementing legislation was required. The U.S. agency primarily responsible for implementing the agreement is the Fish and Wildlife Service.

The range of the Porcupine Caribou Herd is centered on the Porcupine River in the United States and Canada; the herd winters south of the Brooks Range in both nations. The herd of about 120,000 animals provides the staple diet of Gwich'in hunters in Alaska, the Yukon, and the Northwest Territories. It is also the source of cultural tradition and a focus of religious ceremonies. Fearing that oil development in the herd's most frequent calving ground in ANWR's coastal plain area might jeopardize their livelihood and even their culture, the Gwich'in on both sides of the border have vigorously opposed development. Indeed, the concern over the PCH has invigorated cross-border contacts between Gwich'in over the last decade or more.

Under current law, Alaskan Gwich'in would receive relatively little economic benefit from development, successful or otherwise. In contrast, Inuit Natives (primarily from Barrow and Kaktovik) along Alaska's North Slope would receive tax revenues, as well as bonus, royalty, and rent payments if successful development took place on Native-owned subsurface lands within ANWR. As a result of their experience with Pradhoe Bay development, and of its effects on the smaller Central Arctic Herd (CAH), most Inuit feel that ANWR development can proceed without significant risk to the PCH.

The Canadian portion of the PCH calving ground is protected in Ivvavik National Park. While some energy exploration has taken place in the Canadian portion of the calving area, Canadians argue that that activity occurred only before the government was aware of the importance of the area to the PCH. Indeed, some Canadian industry officials now complain of government hostility to development in the northern areas of the country, based on what they perceive as overzealous environmental concerns. Critics counter that the area was not protected until after the area was known to lack commercial energy resources.

The enormous natural gas reserves (over 31 trillion cubic feet) near Prudhoe Bay had been considered uneconomic until recent spikes in natural gas prices. Old plans to run a gas pipeline south are being revived. Estimated costs could be as much as U.S. $20 billion. Three options are widely discussed, two of them with significant Canadian mileage:

- the "over the top" or northern route, east from Prudhoe under the Beaufort Sea, and then south through the Yukon and Northwest Territories, southeast to Alberta and then to markets in the upper Midwest;
- the "Alaska Highway" route, south parallel to the TransAlaska Pipeline System (TAPS), then east to the Highway through the Yukon and British Columbia, and southeast through Alberta to U.S. markets; and
- the "all Alaska" route parallel to TAPS, to a (yet to be built) tanker port for liquefied natural gas, terminating at either Valdez or Cook Inlet.

The Alaska state legislature opposes the first option. Gov. Tony Knowles of Alaska has supported the second option, and on May 6, 2002, leaders in the Alaska House pulled a bill to grant a $600 million tax incentive to construct such a pipeline to the Lower 48.

STATUS OF THE ISSUE

Canadian Prime Ministers have raised the issue of development in the PCH calving range on several occasions over the years, and their government has sent numerous position papers to various U.S. agencies and departments. The Bush Administration strongly supports development of ANWR. The House passed H.R. 4 in August, 2001, with a title that opened the Refuge to energy development. The Senate's version of H.R. 4 does not contain such a provision, and differs from the House bill in many other features. A Murkowski amendment to open the refuge was filibustered; a cloture motion on the amendment was defeated (46 yeas to 54 nays). Many observers predict that a conference committee will have difficulty reconciling the many differences between the two bills.

On the pipeline question, industry has studied the feasibility of various routes; they view the over the top route as the most economical choice, but still say the project is not economic. Both House and Senate versions of H.R. 4 contain a provision forbidding issuance of federal permits, licenses, etc., necessary to build a pipeline following the route over the top. The Senate version also contains loan guarantees, and a tax credit if natural gas prices fall below $3.25 per thousand cubic feet, and other features to encourage development of a natural gas pipeline.

Canada's federal government supports a Canadian route. The Canadian government has not taken a stand on which of the two possible Canadian routes it might prefer; affected provincial governments all support routes through their jurisdictions. The over the top route could make some natural gas deposits in the Yukon and Northwest Territories economically viable, hi either case, Prime Minister Chrétien has expressed Canada's interest in selling more oil and natural gas to meet U.S. energy needs. (Some have argued that this interest has influenced Canadian opposition to ANWR development.)

However, Canada is deeply concerned that the proposed price support in the Senate version of H.R. 4 could not only damage or even end Canadian natural gas sales to the United States, but might also flood western Canada with sufficient natural gas to destroy the area's own natural gas production. In addition, some Canadian critics reportedly claimed that price supports could interfere with free trade and therefore violate NAFTA. U.S. domestic producers in the Lower 48 have also expressed reservations about potential distortions in the natural gas market.

QUESTIONS

1. Canada has argued that the price supports in the Senate version of H.R. 4 would pose a severe threat to the natural gas industry of western Canada. Please explain how it reached that conclusion. Will Canada argue that this move constitutes a violation of NAFTA? Of WTO

agreements? Do affected provincial governments prefer one route over another?
2. How can one reconcile the opposition of the Canadian government to energy development in ANWR (where the PCH calves in most years) to its support of an over the top natural gas pipeline? Would the pipeline be sited to avoid the areas that the PCH tends to use for calving in the years when it does not reach ANWR in time?
3. What energy activities are going on currently in the northern Yukon and the Northwest Territories? What activities have occurred in the last two years?
4. If Congress decides to open ANWR to development, are there specific mitigation practices that Canada is seeking for the protection of caribou? For the protection of other marine or terrestrial species?

INDEX

A

Action Plan, 50
Afghanistan, 2, 7, 8, 11, 13, 15
Africa, 7, 9, 12, 16
agricultural commodities, ix, 17
Air Transport Security Authority, 15
airline safety, 2
Al Qaeda, 11, 15
Alaska, 19, 30, 74, 81-83
Alberta, 2, 4, 13, 22, 83
American Iron and Steel Institute, 34
American Review of Canadian Studies (ARCS), 8, 18
annual budget surpluses, 4
antidumping, 29, 31, 34, 35, 49, 57, 58
Arctic National Wildlife Refuge, (ANWR), 19, 81-85
Asia-Pacific Economic Cooperation, 12
asylum, 15, 66, 70
Attorney General, 66-68
Axworthy, Loyd, 10

B

Bahamas, 48
Balkans, 7
Barbados, 48

Bermuda, 48
Bernard Landry, 6, 23, 24
biometric identifiers, 66, 68
Bloc Québécois (BQ), 3, 22
border crossings, 15, 42, 67
border issues, 49, 67
border management, 42, 66
Border Security and Visa Entry Reform Act, 66
border security, ix, 2, 14, 15, 41, 65, 66
Bosnia, 7, 9
Bouchard, Lucien, 5, 23
Boundary Waters Treaty, 18
Brazil, 48, 50
British Columbia, 4, 16, 30, 42, 74, 75, 83
budget deficits, 2
budget surpluses, 4
Bush Administration, 9, 14, 25, 28, 31, 35, 83
Bush, President, 2, 10, 26, 28, 33-35, 67
Byrd Amendment, 35

C

Calgary declaration, 22
Canada-U.S. Free Trade Agreement, 52

Canada-U.S. Partnership Forum (CUSP), 66
Canada-United States Air Quality Agreement, 19
Canadian Alliance, 3, 71
Canadian economy, 16, 18, 40, 49
Canadian federal milk export subsidy program, 62
Canadian government, 2, 10, 13, 28, 35, 37, 39, 44, 45, 49, 50, 53, 54, 60, 66, 68, 84, 85
Canadian lumber, 29-32
Canadian Radio-Television and Telecommunications Commission (CRTC), 38, 39
Canadian refugee system, 71
Canadian Security Intelligence Service, 9
Canadian Wheat Board (CWB), 55-58
Caribbean free trade area, 48
Caricom, 48
Castro, 13, 14
Central American Common Market, 48
Central Arctic Herd (CAH), 82
Chile, 14, 47, 48
China, 16, 69
Chrétien administration, 22
Chrétien, Jean, 1
Chrétien, Prime Minister, 1, 2, 16, 26, 27, 28, 84
civil liberties, 65
Clarity Bill, 23
Clinton Administration, 6, 34
Clinton, President, 1, 3, 6, 18, 26
Cold War, 7
commerce, 15, 41, 49, 65
common market, 42, 43
construction and demolition (C&D), 78, 79
Costa Rica, 48
countervailing duty, 31, 34, 40, 49, 57, 58

cross-border commerce, 65
Cuba, vii, 13, 14, 25-28
Cuban Democracy Act, 25, 27
Cuban Liberty and Democratic Solidarity Act, 13, 25, 27
cultural identity, 38, 40, 53
cultural industries, 17, 40, 53
cultural issues, 37
cultural sector, 37
customs union, 42
Cyprus, 7
Czech Republic, 10

D

dairy markets, 59
dairy producers, 59
dairy product exports, 61
dairy products, 59-62, 64
defense spending, 7, 8, 9
democracy, 14, 47, 49
Department of Commerce (DOC), 29, 31, 36
detention policies, 72
development box, 52
diaspora nationalism, 70
direct subsidy, 60
Directors Guild of America, 39
Directors Guild of Canada, 39
dispute settlement process, 53, 59
Doha Development Agenda (DDA), 63
Doha Development Round, 51, 52, 54
Doha Ministerial Declaration, 51
dollarization, 44, 45
domestic issues, 2
drug trafficking, 47

E

East Timor, 10
economic development, 13
economic integration, 41, 43, 46

economic reform, 26
economic sanctions, 12, 25
education, 4, 47, 53
Eggleton, Art, 8, 10
El Salvador, 48
election campaigns, 1
employment, 2, 39, 52, 65
energy development, 81, 82, 84, 85
energy resources, 81, 83
Enhanced Border Security and Visa Entry Reform Act, 68
entertainment industries, 17
entry/exit system, 67
Environment Canada, 77, 78
environmental issues, 2, 50
environmental laws, 43
Environmental Protection Agency, 78
environmental protection, 30, 67
Europe, 9, 16, 36, 48, 70
European Free Trade Association, 16
European Union (EU), 10, 27, 33, 36, 43, 51, 58
export sector, 16, 49
export subsidy, 59-63

F

Federal Bureau of Investigation (FBI), 15
federal funding, 4
federalists, 5, 6, 23
Fish and Wildlife Service, 82
fishing companies, 74
foreign affairs, 12
Foreign Extraterritorial Measures Act (FEMA), 27
foreign policy, vii, ix, 1, 11-13, 49
Free Trade Agreement (FTA), 1, 17, 18, 27, 30, 31, 33, 37, 42, 44, 48, 52, 55, 56
Free Trade Area of the Americas (FTAA), 47-50
free trade, 16, 17, 43, 48, 49, 84

G

G-8 summit, 2, 12
G-8, 2, 12, 13
General Agreement on Tariffs and Trade (GATT), 17, 30, 51
General Agreement on Trade in Services (GATS), 53
Germany, 16
goods and services, 17, 37, 43, 44
Graham, Bill, 12, 28
Great Britain, 22, 48
Great Lakes Water Quality Agreement, 18
Guaranteed Income Supplement, 4
Guatemala, 48

H

Haiti, 12
Havana Treaty, 51
hazardous waste, 19, 77, 78
health care, 2, 5, 53
Honduras, 48
host community agreements, 80
human rights, 11, 25, 26
humanitarian aid, 11
Hungary, 10
Hussein, Saddam, 13

I

Iceland, 7
Illegal Immigration and Immigrant Responsibility Act (IIRIRA), 67, 68
immigrants, 15, 68, 69
Immigration and Naturalization Service Data Management and Improvement Act, 67
Immigration and Naturalization Service, 67
Immigration and Refugee Act, 71
immigration, 15, 41-3, 66, 67, 69-72

income taxes, 4
India, 69
inflation, 16, 45
Information Technology Agreement (ITA), 52
intelligence sharing, 65, 66
International Criminal Court (ICC), 14
International Monetary Fund, 26
international organizations, vii, 12
international security, vii, ix
International Trade Commission (ITC), 29-31, 34, 35, 57, 58
international trade, 12, 52
Internet, 39
Iraq, 13

J

Japan, 51, 56, 74
Joint Statement on Cooperation on Border Security and Regional Migration Issues, 15
Joint Strike Fighter program, 9

K

Korean War, 11
Kosovo, 9, 11

L

Latin America, 25, 48, 49
law enforcement, 2, 66, 67
Liberal Party, vii
Liberals, 3, 5, 23
loonie, 16, 44, 45
lower taxes, 5
lumber imports, 29, 30, 31, 32
lumber prices, 31
Luxembourg, 7

M

Macedonia, 9, 10
Manley, John, 12, 27, 44
Martin, Paul, 3, 4
media, 37-39, 53
Memorandum of Understanding (MOU), 30
Mercosur, 48
Mexico, 33-35, 42, 43, 46, 48
Middle East, 7, 9, 71, 81
migration, 66
monetary union, 42, 44, 45
Mulroney, Brian, 1
municipal solid waste (MSW), 78, 79

N

National Association of Wheat Growers, 57
National Missile Defense (NMD), 10
national security, 5, 35, 69
NATO, 7-11
natural gas market, 84
natural gas, 81, 83, 84, 85
Netherlands, 26
New Democratic Party, 4
New International Instrument on Cultural Diversity, 53
New Partnership for Africa's Development, 13
New Zealand, 59, 60, 62, 63
Newfoundland, 4
Nicaragua, 48
non-hazardous waste, 78
North American Aerospace Defense Command (NORAD), 9, 10
North American Free Trade Agreement (NAFTA), 1, 17, 24, 27, 31-34, 37, 38, 40, 42, 46, 48-50, 52, 54, 56, 84
North American integration, 41, 45
North Dakota Wheat Commission (NDWC), 56, 57

Northern Command, 9
Northern Ireland, 13

O

Office of Inspector General (OIG), 65
Old Age Security, 4
Operation Allied Force, 11
Operation Anaconda, 11
Operation Apollo, 11
Operation Enduring Freedom, 11
Organization for Economic Cooperation and Development (OECD), 12, 36
Organization of American States, 48
Ottawa process, 12
Ottawa, vii, 1, 6-10, 12-15, 22, 23

P

Pacific Salmon Commission, 75
Pacific salmon fisheries, 75
Pacific Salmon Treaty, 18, 73, 75
Pacific Salmon, ix, 18, 73, 75
Pakistan, 69
Parti Québécois (PQ), 5, 6, 22, 23
partitioning, 23
Peace Clause, 58
peacekeeping, 7, 9
Pequists, 6, 23
Pettigrew, Pierre, 35
Philippines, 69
pipeline question, 84
Poland, 10
political issues, vii, ix
Porcupine Caribou Herd (PCH), 82, 83, 85
poverty, 47
Prague Summit, 10
progressive conservatives, 3
protectionism, 53
public opinion, 42
public policy, ix

Q

Quad group, 51
Quebec City, 2, 12, 14, 47
Quebec issue, ix, 6, 22
Quebec question, 6, 21, 22
Quebec sovereignty issue, 3
Quebec Summit, 50
Quebeckers, 5, 6, 22, 23
Québécois, 5, 21

R

Reagan, Ronald, 1
Record of Understanding (ROU), 55, 56
referendum, 5, 6, 21-24
refugee claimants, 70-72
refugees, 69, 71
Ressam, Ahmed, 14, 71
Royal Canadian Mounted Police, 12, 15, 67
runaway production, 39, 40
Russia, 16, 26
Rwanda, 7

S

safeguard measures, 35, 36
San Jose Ministerial declaration, 47
Saskatchewan, 4
Screen Actors Guild, 39, 40
Secretary of State Albright, 6
security cooperation, 45
Seniors Benefit, 4
separatists, 5, 22
September 11, vii, 2, 9, 15, 41, 42, 45, 65, 67, 71
Shamrock Summits, 1
Sherritt International, 14, 26
Sinai, 7
small and medium enterprises (SMEs), 53
Smart Border declaration, 15

Smart Border Declaration, 42
smart-border, 66
social programs, 4, 5
softwood lumber, 2, 17, 29, 30, 31, 32, 43, 46, 53, 54
Solid Waste Disposal Act, 78
solid waste, 19, 77, 78, 79
Somalia, 7
South America, 48
Southern Cone Common Market, 48
Sovereigntists, 23
sovereignty, 3, 5, 6, 9, 14, 21, 23, 24, 28, 41, 42, 45
Soviet Union, 7
Special Milk Classes Scheme (SMCS), 60, 61
Stabilization Force (SFOR), 9
Standing Committee on Foreign Affairs and International Trade (SCFAIT), 52, 53
State Department, 7, 17, 26
state trading enterprise(s) (STE(s)), 55, 57, 58
steel imports, 33-35
steel industry, 34, 36
Suez Crisis, 7
Summit of the Americas, 12, 14, 27, 47
Supreme Court, 23, 71

T

Taliban, 11
tariff-rate quota (TRQ), 56-58, 60, 61
tariffs, 33, 34, 35, 36, 42, 49, 52, 54, 60
tax cuts, 5
taxation, 4
Team Canada, 16
terrorism, vii, 2, 8, 9, 11, 13, 15, 45
terrorist groups, 72
terrorists, 13, 15, 71, 72
Toronto Stock Exchange, 44
tourism, 67

Trade Act of 1974, 33, 56
trade agreements, 49, 54, 58
trade analysts, 58
trade disputes, 18, 41, 46, 50, 54
trade issues, 17
trade liberalization, 52, 64
Trade Promotion Authority, 50, 54
trade relief, 34, 35
TransAlaska Pipeline System (TAPS), 82, 83
Trudeau, Prime Minister, 26

U

U.N. War Crimes Tribunal, 12
U.S. Canada Free Trade Agreement, 17, 44
U.S. Coalition for Fair Lumber Imports, 31
U.S. Customs, 15
U.S. Department of Agriculture (USDA), 55, 78
U.S. entertainment industry, 37
U.S. farm bill, 46, 54
U.S. Federal Reserve, 45
U.S. film industry, 39
U.S. International Trade Commission (USITC), 29, 30, 34, 56, 57
U.S. law, 25, 27
U.S. lumber industry, 29, 31
U.S. Members of Congress, ix
U.S. Non-Immigrant Visa system, 70
U.S. property, 26
U.S. State Department, 7, 17
U.S. steel industry, 34, 35
U.S. trade law, 32, 34, 35, 40
U.S. Trade Representative (USTR), 56, 57, 58
U.S. Wheat Associates, 57
U.S.-Canada Free Trade Agreement (CUSTA), 1, 37, 55
U.S.-Canadian agricultural trade, 55, 56
undercutting prices, 57

Index

unemployment, 16
United Nations, 7, 9, 12
United States Customs Service, 67
United Steelworkers Union (USWA), 34
Uruguay Round Agreement, 58
USA PATRIOT Act, 66

V

Venezuela, 48
visa requirements, 72

W

Warsaw Pact, 7
waste shipments, 77
weapons of mass destruction, 13
wheat prices, 55, 58
wheat trading, 56
World Trade Center, 2
World Trade Organization (WTO), 17, 18, 27, 31-35, 37, 50, 51, 54, 57-64, 84
WTO Agreement on Agriculture, 61
WTO Agriculture Agreement, 60
WTO compliance review, 62